The Phenomenal Seed

How to sow financially into the Kingdom of God
and receive your miracle

Timothy Flemming, Jr.

The Phenomenal Seed

How to sow financially into the Kingdom of God
and receive your miracle

Timothy Flemming, Jr.

T&J Publishers
A SMALL INDEPENDENT PUBLISHER WITH A BIG VOICE

Printed in the United States of America by
T&J Publishers (Atlanta, GA.)
www.TandJPublishers.com

All Scriptures are from the King James Version (KJV), the New Living Translation (NLT), the New International Version (NIV), and the New American Standard Bible (NASB)

Cover design by Timothy Flemming, Jr.
(T&J Publishers)

Book format and layout by Timothy Flemming, Jr.
(T&J Publishers)

ISBN: 978-0-9994121-0-7

To contact author, go to:
www.TimothyFlemmingJr.com
Facebook: Timothy Flemming, Jr.
Instagram: Timothy Flemming, Jr.
Linkedin: Timothy Flemming, Jr.
TJPublishers@gmail.com

Acknowledgments

First, I would like to thank the one from whom all good and perfect gifts flow: my Lord and Savior, Jesus the Christ. The ability to write, ability to think, ability to do the things that I do all come from Him. He gave me this gift, and I owe every ounce of happiness and success to Him.

Secondly, I would like to thank my lovely wife, Jackie. You are my best friend and greatest supporter. Nothing in this world compares to the beauty you possess both within and without, and you are invaluable, incomparable, and unique in every way. I thank God for the gift of you and for the three wonderful ones you have given me: my oldest son Timothy III, my daughter Timera, and my youngest son Jeremiah, each of whom are like candescent candles glowing in the darkness, providing me with such great inspiration in my life.

To my parents, I thank you and love you both. Thank you for your prayers, support, hard work and sacrifice in helping me to become the man I have become. You mean so much to me.

To all of my family members (my brother Kenneth and my nephew Aric, as well as others), thank you for your support and encouragement.

Lastly, to all of my friends and supporters, thank you for your words of encouragement, prayers, and support. I can't tell you how much these things mean to me.

"The seed that you sow never leaves your life - it simply goes into your future. When you release what's in your hand, I (God) will release what's in my hand."

—Dr. Mike Murdoch.

Table of Contents

Introduction

It's A Divine Law

One of my favorite childhood movies was *The Goonies*. In this 1985 film, a group of youngsters, hoping to save their homes from foreclosure and demolition at the hands of an expanding country club, went searching for the hidden treasure that was rumored to have been left behind by a legendary 17th century pirate named One-Eyed Willy. The youngsters risked life and limb to find the treasure: being chased by a group of criminals and dodging booby traps along the way. The lure of precious gold and silver was worth the risk.

In the mid 1800's, the state of California was prime real estate in America thanks to James W. Marshall, a saw-mill operator who stumbled upon gold in Coloma, California, one day while building a mill for his employer. Following Marshall's discovery of gold, hundreds of thousands of men, women, and children migrated to California in search of gold in what became known as the California Gold Rush. People loaded up into their caravans and headed west in an effort to find gold; they risked traveling through dangerous territories filled with robbers and murderers just to strike it rich. Gold is so important to most people that they will risk their lives just to obtain it; they'll give up everything just to get their hands on it. Did you know that there is something far more valuable than gold? There is. It's called *wisdom*.

The wisest and wealthiest man to have ever walked the earth instructed us to pursue after wisdom as if it is hidden treasure in Proverbs 2:4. He said, "...seek her as silver, and search for her as for hid treasures..." According to King Solomon, the writer of this proverb, we should be treasure hunters—our treasure being wisdom rather than gold. This is an adventure; it's the greatest adventure you'll ever take. Like the youngsters in *The Goonies*, you have some sinister characters on your trail trying to stop you from obtaining this prized possession: I'm referring to Satan and his agents. There are booby traps to watch out for like the counterfeit wisdom of the world and there is spiritual deception at every turn, but the prize is worth it. God's wisdom is worth your life and limbs. What is wisdom? It's the understanding of God's divine laws which govern our world and universe. Knowing these divine laws is more rewarding than acquiring all of the gold and silver in the world.

Today, we are familiar with certain of God's divine

laws known as the laws of nature thanks to physicists. When Isaac Newton observed an apple one day falling from a tree and onto the ground, he hypothesized that there exist laws that govern the forces of nature. From this experience, he famously proposed what we now know as the Law of Gravity. Newton had simply joined the ranks of the many other great thinkers that had preceded him in making the discovery that *nothing just happens*—that every occurrence in life is determined by some pre-existing natural law.

What goes up must come down Newton deduced upon seeing that apple fall. But there are other laws of nature that have been discovered besides the Law of Gravity. For example, there is The Law of Causation, which states every cause has an effect and vice versa; there's The Law of Conservation of Energy, which states that matter and energy are neither created nor destroyed over time, but they simply change forms; there's The Law of Motion (Inertia), which says an object at rest will remain at rest and an object in motion will remain in motion with the same speed and in the same direction unless it is acted upon by some outside force (I know plenty of people who struggle with this one); and there are so many more natural laws to add to this list. But, to truthful, you don't have to be a physicist nor be educated to realize there are laws that govern our world and universe. Grandma would tell you, "Child, what goes around, comes around. What goes up must come down. Be careful, now, cause you gonna' reap what you sow." She knew just as much about divine/natural laws as Newton and Einstein.

Where did grandma get her wisdom from? She got it from the one book that bears God's signature: the Bible. And by the way, if you think the Bible is some mystical book that lacks scientific facts, think again. It contains hundreds of scientific facts our scientists didn't discover until recently. For example, Job 26:7 revealed to us that God "suspends the earth over nothing (i.e. gravity)" thousands of years before Newton was born and Isaiah told us God sits upon "the circle of the earth" thousands of years before the brightest and smartest among us discovered that the earth wasn't flat like a pancake (Isaiah 40:22). There are hundreds of scientific facts contained in the Bible from the laws of Thermodynamics to the revelation that light travels in a path and can be divided to springs at the bottom of the ocean which scientists didn't discover until the 1970s to micro organisms to the expanding universe revelation (long before Einstein discovered it) to the incalculable number of stars, the continental drift, the Ice Age, blood being the life source of the body, the Hydrological Cycle, sanitation laws, dietary laws, etc.

King Solomon's knew the value of wisdom (the understanding of God's divine laws). Solomon asked God for wisdom as opposed to money and revenge, and God gave it to him. Some of this wisdom Solomon shares with us in the wisdom books of the Bible (Proverbs, Ecclesiastes, Song of Solomon). This is what the book of 1 Kings says about the wisdom of Solomon:

> 1 Kings chapter four tells us that Solomon was wiser than all of the "men of the East and the wise men of Egypt. He was wiser than anyone else, including Ethan the Ezrahite and the sons of Mahol—Heman, Calcol, and Darda. His fame spread throughout all the surrounding nations. He composed some 3,000 proverbs and wrote 1,005 songs. He could speak with authority about all kinds of plants, from the great cedar of Lebanon to the tiny hyssop that grows from cracks in a wall. He could also speak about animals, birds, small creatures, and fish" (vs. 30-33, NLT).

Great kings from every corner of the world would descend upon that little piece of land known as Israel just to sit at the feet of King Solomon as he shared revelations of divine laws; and by the way, these kings, queens, and emissaries didn't approach Solomon empty-handed; they brought many gifts with them in caravans: gold, silver, spices, fabrics and more. This is how Solomon gained his wealth. People with money paid top dollar just to hear him speak and reveal to them the mysteries of God's divine laws, mysteries that contained information on health and healing, science, cosmology and so much more.

If you had all of the money in the world but was sick and dying slowly and painfully from cancer, would you be willing to spend every dime you have just for a cure? What if God shared with you a natural cure for cancer by revealing to you a supreme understanding of the properties of all plants and herbs? With this knowledge, do you think you'd become rich? I guarantee you that you'd become one of the most sought after individuals on the face of the earth due to the information you possess. Wisdom attracts money because it enables you to answer questions, meet needs, and solve problems. This is why you can't place a price tag on wisdom. You can't eat money; but with God's wisdom, you will know how to grow fruits and vegetables in a desert, and that kind of knowledge is worth all of the silver and gold in the world.

How much do you think your net-worth would be if you were the only person on the earth who knew the cure for AIDS? Do you think this special information would cause your net-worth to surpass that of Bill Gates', Warren Buffet's, and even the combined wealth of the Rothchilds and Rockerfellers at the height of their empire? Without a doubt: yes! Just that one revelation alone would make you the richest man on the planet. Now, imagine knowing the cures for every disease on the planet...and then some. Money can't compare to the value of God's wisdom.

During the gold rush of the 1800's, people were willing to kill and steal just for gold. Imagine if people knew the value of wisdom: they'd fight, scratch and claw just to get a seat in church to hear the wisdom of God being shared by the ministers of God; they'd be moved by a sense of desperation for this knowledge and understanding, a desperation that surpasses any quest for gold. But how many people do you know who are desperate for wisdom?

Solomon's wisdom enabled him to speak on every law that governs nature; human nature included. With ease, Solomon would have been able to put to shame the world's leading botanists, geologists, cosmologists, zoologists, herbologists, marine biologists, biologists, psychologists, ecologists, economists, and all other *ologists* (experts); he even possessed knowledge of spiritual laws and realities, which many of the ancients, especially the ancient Egyptians, were quite fond of. Of the many divine laws Solomon gave us, here are a few of the simpler ones he provided for our daily living in the book of Proverbs:

- Laziness leads to poverty (10:4, 13:4, 20:4, 20:13)
- Stinginess leads to poverty (28:22, 28:27, 22:9, 21:13)
- Alcoholism and addiction to pleasure leads to poverty and shame (23:20-21, 23:29-35, 21:17)
- Hanging with evil and perverse people will damage your character and reputation and even cut your life short (1:8-19, 13:20, 22:24-25, 27:6)
- Not listening to sound counsel will lead to poverty and failure (12:15, 11:14, 15:22)
- Not pursuing knowledge will lead to failure and shame (1:5, 1:22, 1:29, 18:15, 15:14)
- Not being informed before speaking and offering your opinion about something will destroy your credibility and make you look like a fool (13:16, 17:12, 18:13)
- Not heeding correction will lead to shame and failure in life (12:1-28, 15:32)

- Sleeping with another person's spouse will lead to shame, destruction, and even death (5:3-22, 6:24-29, 6:32)
- Pride leads to destruction (11:22, 16:5, 16:18, 29:23)

Alongside the many principles Solomon stated concerning our daily living, he shared one in Proverbs 3:9-10, which is a big key to financial wealth and prosperity. Solomon wrote,

> "Honor the LORD from your wealth
> And from the *first of all your produce*;
> So your barns will be filled with plenty
> And your vats will overflow with new wine." (NASB)

This is the Law of Sacrifice—put another way, this is the Law of Giving (sometimes called The Law of Sowing and Reaping). Solomon explains here that no financial blessing comes without there first being a financial sacrifice. As we go throughout this book, we will take a look at some of the financial sacrifices listed in Scripture that we need to make... and how to make them. For the time being, just understand that there's a divine law that governs financial prosperity. It doesn't matter how much you wish for something; if you are oblivious of the laws that govern what you're wishing for, you'll never receive it. You can wish to soar like an eagle through the air, but if you don't understand aeronautics, you won't be soaring anywhere. Likewise, understand that financial prosperity operates on pre-existing laws. So, you can wish for money all you want, but if you don't understand the way money is handled, transferred, obtained, is to be managed, etc., then you won't receive any or keep any for long. Your understanding of the laws of wealth, sowing and reaping, and giving determines whether or not you will receive the financial prosperity you desire...and need. And as Solomon points out here, honoring God with your tithe (one tenth of your earnings, formerly taken as a tax for the support of the church and clergy) is crucial as it pertains to securing wealth for yourself and your household. This law is as old as Methusalem—no, literally! Abraham was a tither long before there was a Mosaic Law. Tithing was a well-established practice in the ancient world, especially during the time of Abraham, and perhaps much earlier than that. In fact, concerning the laws or commandments of the Lord, if ever anyone claims that Abraham and his descendants did not have the "laws" of God to live by, then ask that person to explain Genesis 26:5, which says this:

> "Because that Abraham obeyed my voice, and kept my charge, *my commandments*, my statutes, and *my laws*."

God gave Abraham "laws" and "commandments" to abide by. I bet you that among those laws and commandments was the instruction to tithe and render offerings unto the Lord.

Not only did Abraham have knowledge and possession of the laws and the commandments (God's divine order) of the Lord, but so did the king he tithed to, Melchizedek; for, the Bible proclaims that Melchizedek was both the king and priest of Salem (later called Jeru-salem). As king, Melchizedek was responsible for enforcing the civil laws of the land, but as priest he was responsible for enforcing the spiritual and ceremonial laws of God in the land. Never in the history of the earth has man been without the laws and commandments of God. God has—and always will—have a priest (Godly representative in the earth) and a people to abide by His laws and commandments, which are just external expressions of His personality and character. Basically, God will always make sure there's someone available to do things HIS WAY and to teach others to do the same.

It's in God's nature to give; therefore, God says that in order to receive you must first give. You can't reap unless you first sow. If you're hoping to have a child, you must first sow seed in a woman's womb. If you're looking to create a harvest, you must first sow seed in the ground. If you want financial prosperity, be prepared to sacrifice financially. It's a divine law. This is the very law Solomon followed in order to secure the wisdom of God in his life:

> "The most important of these places of worship was at Gibeon, so the king went there and *sacrificed 1,000 burnt offerings*. That night the LORD appeared to Solomon in a dream, and God said, 'What do you want? Ask, and I will give it to you!'" (NLT)

Solomon didn't just pray for wisdom; he sowed for it. Solomon sowed financially into the Kingdom of God at the altar at Gibeon, and only behind this sacrificial act did God pay Solomon a visit in the night. In Acts 10:31, a Greek named Cornelius received a similar response. God sent the Apostle Peter to this gentile to share with him this message and also pray for him and his family to be filled with the Holy Spirit:

> "'Cornelius, your prayer has been heard and *your alms have been remembered before God...*" (NASB)

God not only considered Cornelius' prayers, but his many financial sacrifices when deciding to bless him. Prayer and financial giving go together. If you're wondering why some people pray but still can't receive the breakthroughs they're looking for, first examine their giving.

In the case of both Solomon and Cornelius, there's a common denomenator: both men gave to God and both of them received divine favor in return. Giving sets you up for the favor of God. Giving draws God's attention towards us. When you have God's attention, that is better than having Mark Cuban sitting in the living room of your house with his checkbook open eager to finance your dreams. The favor of the Lord is more valuable than all of the money in the world as Solomon experienced. Due to the favor of God in his life, Solomon's net-worth reached over $2.2 trillion as reported in an article entitled *The 20 richest people of all time* posted on www.msn.com. And not only that, but God's favor brings happiness and prosperity to every aspect of your life, and not just your finances (Proverbs 10:22; 3 John 1:2).

The Bible tells us to honor God with our money and He will bless us; it doesn't say present to God our wish-lists and expect Him to do as we ask. God isn't our servant. The Bible declares when we honor God by giving Him our best, He will give us His best in return. There must first be a sacrifice made. Regarding this matter, God leads by example; for, He was the first to make the ultimate sacrifice: He gave us His best roughly two-thousand years ago when He sent His own Son, Jesus, to earth to be the sacrifice for our sins. Jesus was the payment for our ransom (1 Timothy 2:6). Jesus "redeemed" (to gain or regain possession of something in exchange for payment) us from the hands of Satan by His blood (Ephesians 1:7). Jesus' blood was payment for a debt owed by each one of us for our sins, but not only that; Jesus, according to the Apostle Paul, was the "seed" God planted in the earth to produce a harvest of Believers. Paul said that Jesus was the "firstborn of many brothers and sisters" in Romans 8:29. God sowed in order that He might reap. God made the ultimate sacrifice. God lives by His own law—the Law of Sacrifice—which He demonstrated to us repeatedly in the Bible. Now, it is time for us to follow His example.

I'm glad you are holding this book. You are now on an expedition to discover something far more valuable than gold; you are about to discover a divine law that will change your financial situation...and ultimately, your life.

Chapter One

Why God Talks So Much About Money

The Bible offers around five-hundred verses on prayer and even fewer verses on faith; however, it offers more than two-thousand verses on money. Apparently, money is an important subject in the Bible. But the main question that I hear so many people ask is, "Why money? Why is money such a big issue to God?" When teaching on the principle of the tithe and the seed offering, I've heard people ask, "Why do I have to give money in order to get a blessing from God? Isn't that like buying a blessing?" First of all, you're not paying for a blessing. You can't afford what God truly desires to give you, nor can you afford what He has already provided for us: life, salvation through Christ Jesus, peace of mind, etc. But God challenges us in the area of financial giving because money reveals something important about our character and true spiritual condition. Furthermore, when we complain about being challenged to give financially before God releases blessings to us, this attitude is a reflection of the type of thinking that keeps people in financial bondage: it is the idea that no one should have the right to demand anything from us but we should have the right to demand things from others; it's the idea that being challenged to make a sacrifice is unfair even though it's completely okay for us to expect others to make sacrifices for us. Basically, complaining about having to give financial reveals our selfish motives.

Let me share with you a few reasons why God places so much emphasis on money:

1. God demands a financial sacrifice from us because by doing so we learn how to honor and reverence Him. The Bible says this in Deuteronomy 14:22-23:

> "You must set aside a tithe of your crops—one-tenth of all the crops you harvest each year. Bring this tithe to the designated place of worship—the place the LORD your God chooses for his name to be honored—and eat it there in his presence. This applies to your tithes of grain, new wine, olive oil, and the firstborn males of your flocks and herds. Doing this will teach you always to fear the LORD your God."

The word "fear" in the Hebrew is *yare'* and it means "to

reverence (to feel deep respect or admiration for something or someone)." The tithe was required by God to be given first and from the best of the Israelites' crops and livestock; through this system, the Israelites would always be reminded that all of their blessings came from God and they'd also remember to keep Him first and make Him a priority.

In America, we are trained to honor the government due to the fact that we must pay our taxes before we do anything else with our money; in fact, taxes are taken out of our paychecks before we even receive them. Through taxation, the US government is able to continue on with many of its operations (funding social programs, paying its employees, funding the military, providing aid to our allies, etc.). In the Kingdom of God, things work the same way. Through our tithes and offerings, the church is able to continue on with its many operations (fund its outreach activities, spread the gospel through media, provide for those in need, pay those who work full-time in the ministry, and more). Unlike the US government, however, the church doesn't throw people in prison for not paying their fair share. There's no such thing as an Ecclesiastical IRS (Internal Revenue Service) agency. The government *forces* you to honor it; but God, on the other hand, *asks* us to honor Him. The US government takes their money from the top without our consent; God, on the other hand, asks us to make Him a priority. But then again, the government can only put you in jail while God, on the other hand, can cast you into hell for all eternity. The Bible tell us that thieves, among other things, will not inherit the Kingdom of God in 1 Corinthians 6:10. This indicates to us that non-tithing is not only a sin, but it's an act that can actually jeopardize our souls, being that God considers it to be an act of stealing from Him. (Side note: In this passage of Scripture, Paul was discouraging Believers against immorality by explaining that every "wrongdoer" will be judged for their deeds. This warning is to Believers, not sinners.)

In Malachi 1:6-8, God said,

> The LORD of Heaven's Armies says to the priests: "A son honors his father, and a servant respects his master. If I am your father and master, where are the honor and respect I deserve? You have shown contempt for my name! "But you ask, 'How have we ever shown contempt for your name?' "You have shown contempt by offering defiled sacrifices on my altar. "Then you ask, 'How have we defiled the sacrifices?' "You defile them by saying the altar of the LORD deserves no respect. When you give blind animals as sacrifices, isn't that wrong? And isn't it wrong to offer animals that are crippled and diseased? Try giving gifts like that to your governor, and see how pleased he is!" says the LORD of Heaven's Armies. (NLT)

God knows that we invest into the things that we value the most; therefore, in an attempt to see where our hearts truly lie, He sits back and watches to see what we invest into the most and He observes the attitudes we have when it comes to giving to Him. God is watching us! Do we make financing the things of God a priority in our lives? Honor operates off of the principle of prioritizing. Whoever we honor the most we will pay the most attention to, give the most consideration to, express the most respect and appreciation for, and submit to. Do we truly honor God? Do we complain about paying our tithes to the one who gives us breath but rejoice when it comes to going to musical concerts put on by secular musicians who care nothing about us and whose concert ticket prices may range into the hundreds and thousands of dollars? What is your attitude when it comes to financing the things that matter most to God? If the desires of God's heart aren't important to you, then why should the desires of your heart matter to Him? This is the very perspective of God as expressed in Malachi 1:9, where the Bible says, "Go ahead, beg God to be merciful to you! But when you bring that kind of offering, why should he show you any favor at all?' asks the LORD of Heaven's Armies."

In Haggai 1:4, God complained again about the attitudes of those who claimed to make Him their top priority:

> "Why are you living in luxurious houses while my house lies in ruins?" (NLT)

Was God really complaining about a tabernacle (tent)? Did God even need one? No. Truthfully, the God who sits upon the glorious throne of heaven where the streets are paved with gold had no need for an earthly tabernacle in a barren desert. God wasn't concerned with the tabernacle; He was concerned with the Israelites' lack of regard for the things that represented His presence. I can hear you retorting "Oh, the church is just 'a building.'" True! But it's a building that represents the presence of God in the earth; it's a place that God chose to place His name and reputation on just like in ancient Israel where God chose to place His name and reputation on the tabernacle. With that being said, the church house is more than just "a building"; it's the house of God in the earth, a place that has been consecrated for His presence and use; it's the place the Lord our God has chosen for His name to be honored. If you want God to bless your house, then you need to make blessing and preserving God's house your top priority. Furthermore, the church is the body of Christ; so, if you bless God's people, you are blessing that which God deems most important to Him. This is why the Apostle Paul wrote, "Therefore, whenever we have the opportunity, we should do good to everyone—especially to those in the family of faith" (Galatians 6:10, NLT)

God simply wants to know what your priorities are. These are God's top priorities: saving the lost through the preaching of the gospel (Mark 16:15), meeting the needs of His people (2 Corinthians 9:12-13), preserving the Jewish Nation of Israel (Zechariah 2:8, Romans 11), and preparing the church for His imminent return (1 Thessalonians 4). These should be your top priorities. This is what the Apostle Paul meant when he wrote, "Set your affection on things above, not on things on the earth" in Colossians 3:2. Paul was saying we must give top priority status to that which God makes a priority; he was not telling us to walk around daydreaming about heaven all day while wallowing in escapism. We shouldn't be focused on leaving this world; but rather, we should focus on doing the "work" of ministry in the earth because there is a lot that must still be done.

2. Money reveals where our faith truly lies. Oh, we just love to sing songs about how we love and trust God and how He is our everything. That's fine. But there's just one thing: the true state of your heart isn't revealed by your lip service; it's revealed by your use of money. Don't believe me? Well, let us see what God says about the use of money:

- *Matthew 6:24*—"No one can serve two masters. For you will hate one and love the other; you will be devoted to one and despise the other. You cannot serve both God and money" (NLT). Notice here that Jesus is able to determine who is your master by who you serve. The word "serve" in this verse is rendered *douleuō* in the Greek, and it is defined as "to be a slave to; be in bondage to." Jesus states here that a man can either be a slave to (be the sole property of; be under the control and power of) God or money, but not both.

  Have you ever been in a position where you heard the Holy Spirit instructing you to give financially, but at the same time, a ton of fears and concerns began to flood your soul, causing you to suddenly become reluctant to obey God? The moment God told you to give, you suddenly began to think about the bills, that outfit you wanted to buy, that trip you wanted to take, etc. But none of these things popped up in your mind when you were about to spend money on other things, things you wanted to get and do. Money has a voice. It talks. When you are about to obey God, that's precisely when money will whisper in your ear and remind you about all of the other things you said you needed and wanted so that you'll become hesitant to give as God commanded you. This is what Jesus meant when He said we can't be slaves to money and God at the same time. Either you're going to silence the voice of your flesh and obey God despite how things look in the natural or you're going to surrender your will to money and disobey God out of fear.

What are we saying to God when we refuse to let go of the cash when the Holy Spirit is urging us to? We're telling God that we don't trust Him—we don't believe that He will take care of us, that He truly understands our needs, and that He is dependable; we're also saying He's incapable of meeting our needs; we call Him a liar. We've communicated to God that we trust money more than Him, which is the same as exalting money to the status of master in our lives over God. Is there any wonder why God will challenge us to give the same way He did the rich young ruler in Matthew chapter 19—where

Jesus challenged the young wealthy man to sell all of his possessions and then give the money to the poor and seek to amass wealth eternally in heaven? Jesus didn't tell all of His disciples to sell all of their possessions and give the money to the poor, so why did He instruct the rich young ruler to do so? It is because Jesus wanted to see if this young man would do as Abraham did and be willing to give up the thing that he valued the most just to prove he loved God more; also, Jesus wanted to challenge him to give up the thing that had become his god: his money. When we can turn our backs on money and give as God instructs us to when He instructs us to, we are proving that money is not our master. When God is confident that money is not your master, then He'll feel comfortable with trusting you with His blessings.

- *1 Timothy 6:10*—"For the love of money is the root of all kinds of evil. And some people, craving money, have wandered from the true faith and pierced themselves with many sorrows" (NLT). It is possible to profess with your mouth that you love God while proving through your actions that you are actually in love with money. With God, it's not about what we say, but what we do that matters.

In 2 Corinthians 8:8, the Apostle Paul urged the Christians in Corinth to "prove the sincerity" of their love through their giving; and in verse 24, Paul urged those Christians to "show them [the needy Christians in

Jerusalem] your love" through giving rather than mere talk. You show love to others by giving generously to them; and in the same manner, that's how you prove to God how much you love Him. It's normal to feel nervous when it comes to making significant financial sacrifices to God. Our flesh will always attempt to dissuade us from making such sacrifices. But a genuine love for God has the tendency to overpower such an apprehension, thereby enabling us to give as instructed by God.

With that being said, the flip-side of this coin is the "love of money," which is where money becomes your #1 driving force in life. When a person is in love with money, all of their decisions are dictated by the dollar; they're motivated by money in every situation; money is their primary goal in life. Some people will choose a higher paying job that will wreak havoc on their families just because of . . . money. Some people center their college education only around the degrees that promise to pay them the most money, caring nothing about the fact that their true passions may not rest in their selected fields. Some people, because they're in love with money so badly, will cut corners, lie, cheat, steal, and even kill just to get it, not caring about the ramifications of their selfish actions; they're simply driven like mindless zombies by an insatiable appetite for money, willing to sacrifice any relationship for the dollar . . . including a relationship with God. To this, Jesus asked the golden question: "For what shall it profit a man, if he shall gain the whole world, and lose his own soul?" (Mark 8:36). The love of money always causes you to make decisions out of alignment with God's divine will and jeopardize your eternal soul. Don't let your ultimate motivation in life for doing anything be money; instead, be motivated by the desire to please God and put a smile on His face. When faced with a tough decision, don't consider how much money you might gain or lose; instead, consider whether or not your actions will procure the favor of God in your life or cause you to lose favor with Him.

- *Matthew 6:21*—"For where your treasure is, there shall your heart be also." The word "treasure" is translated *thēsauros* in the Greek and it means "the place in which good and precious things are collected and laid up; things laid up in a treasury." Therefore, Jesus was saying that which you pursue after the most is your treasure, and that's where your heart is. If you want to know where your heart really lies, think about what you focus on the most, what you obsess about the most, what you spend every waking moment thinking about the most. What fascination colors your day? When God wants to locate your heart, He knows where to look: the place of your deepest longing. He looks at what preoccupies your mind. We don't devote nearly as much time to the pursuit of God as we do the pursuit of money and material possessions. Sure, we must work so that we can eat and take care of basic expenses, but there's a difference between focusing on getting money in order to take care of certain needs and obsessing over money and material things.

I once heard Pastor Andy Stanley, pastor of North Point Community Church, say in a sermon on financial giving that the true condition of a person's heart can be determined by their bank statement. Examine a person's bank statement and you'll see not just where all of their money goes, but what they value the most. I'd imagine that God will occasionally log into our online bank accounts and take a look at our bank statements. He looks and notices that, aside from our utilities, we spent hundreds or thousands of dollars on ourselves—our looks, our clothes, leisure activities, playtime, etc.—but then, we'll only give five dollars in church . . . maybe ten if we were feeling especially giddy that morning. I know God reads our mail and looks at our bank statements. He has to...when you think about the fact that He's always been intimately involved with and concerned about all of our earthly affairs. If God is so in-tune with our lives that He literally knows the number of hairs on the tops of our heads as explained in Matthew 10:30—and knowing how some of us tend to stress our hair out, that would mean God would have to do a recount almost daily—then He also knows about our financial standing. He knows without a doubt. And not only that, but He sees. He sees what's of great value to us by keeping close tabs on our spending patterns and habits. For most of us, this is how our spending goes: we give a lot to the world, a lot to ourselves, and a little to God, and then we expect little from the world, even less from ourselves, but a lot from God. But just as God stated in our earlier passage from Malachi 1:9, why should He value us and show us favor when we don't value Him? If we choose not to draw close to God, He will be stand-off-ish with us too according to James 4:8. If we show God that we aren't interested in Him, then He'll demonstrate a lack of interest in us also according to Hosea 4:6. In Acts 10:34, the Apostle Peter said this: "...Of a truth I perceive that God is no respecter of persons..." That's in the King James Version. I like the New International Version (NIV) which says, "I now realize how true it is that God does not show favoritism..." God doesn't discriminate. He doesn't give to one man because He carries an affinity for that person and then reject and deny another because of some preconceived notion or personal prejudice. No! Everyone has the same chance to be blessed or cursed by God. No one is special or unique in this respect. Peter went on to say, "but accepts from every nation the one who fears him and does what is right" (vs. 35, NIV). Some people are more highly favored and blessed by God because they chose to sacrifice more to and for God: they gave Him more of their time, more of their will, more of their heart and soul, and sacrificed more financially for God's Kingdom. As Paul stated in 2 Corinthians 9, when God sees a person giving "abundantly" from their heart with a "cheerful" spirit, God will likewise respond and bless that individual abundantly and with gladness. God responds to you and your attitude. If I were you, I'd do my best to communicate to God that He is the most important thing in your life, and I would start today by examining your treasury to determine what you really value the most.

3. Money advances God's Kingdom in the earth. Joel Richardson, Bible prophecy expert and author, while a guest on The Jim Bakker Show, revealed this startling revelation regarding why Islam has become perhaps the fastest growing religion in the world and is primed to take over the Christian nations at the rate it's going:

> "If you take all of the money that we spend as Protestants to spread the gospel, it's roughly 1.2 billion dollars a year. Saudi Arabia spends that much every three months and it has for the past forty years to spread not just Islam, [but] Salafi, Wahabi Islam: that's Al Queada, that's ISIS, that's Boko Haram, that's Abu Sayyab, that's Al Shabaab. These are the sickest, most twisted."

What Protestant Christianity spends in a year to spread the gospel Islam spends in a month to spread its message. Who do you suppose is getting their message out quicker? And who do you think will cover more territory with their message? That's a no brainer: Islam! It's not that Islam offers more than Christianity and is therefore more appealing; it's just that Islam spends more than Christianity and is therefore more visible in many parts of the world. They spend more money on television ads and programming and they donate huge sums of money to top colleges and universities in the west such as Harvard, Berkeley, Cornell, Princeton, Rutgers, Oxford, Cambridge and more just to influence the minds of the youth in these schools. Because of their financial donations these schools have developed entire Islamic studies programs and centers dedicated to the propagation of Islam in the west. Should we be surprised to know that the biggest promoters of BDS (which stands for Boycotts, Divestments, and Sanctions against the Jewish State of Israel) are America's top colleges and universities? Our college campuses are rife with antisemitism thanks to the influence of Islamic provocateurs who've gained influence over these institutions simply by donating millions of dollars to them.

When Solomon wrote "money answereth all things" in Ecclesiastes 10:19, he was simply explaining to us that money enables us to accomplish whatever goals we need to accomplish. Regarding evangelism, say you desire to share the gospel with others; let's consider the cost: you need to pay for tracks to pass out, you have to buy those Bibles you intend to give away for free (the people printing the Bibles must be paid); you need gas for the vans, which takes money; you need food and other supplies to give away to those in need, all of which takes money; you and your ministry team must be able to evangelize without worrying about how you are going to eat, where you're going to sleep, etc., and all of this takes money. You want to share your message over television? Well, I hope you have a money tree growing in your back yard. If not, then realize that television is very expensive. The cameramen have to be paid. The sound technicians have to be paid. The people editing the programming must be paid. The make-up artist making you camera ready have to get paid. The stylist must be paid. Many others who are involved in helping that network station to run must be paid. The camera equipment, soundboards, mixers, lighting, software, props, etc. that's used to create that television program cost an arm and a leg. And we're not even talking about the basic utilities that the facility must pay for on a monthly basis: power, gas, water, etc. And neither are we talking about the expense you and your team will undertake just to dig wells in lands where people are suffering drought conditions, provide food on a large scale for people who're starving and have no access to food, provide medical relief to people suffering in territories where they don't have any access to medicine, etc. It takes money to get supplies, move supplies, and even properly distribute supplies. And that is just the tip of the iceberg.

I once encountered a man who complained about how much money churches were taking up on Sunday mornings. He even complained about the pastors' salaries at some of these ministries, which he had surmised based on the types of cars and houses they lived in. Sure, he had never read in the Bible where the Apostle Paul explained that "the Lord has commanded that those who preach the gospel should receive their living from the gospel" in 1 Corinthians 9:14; nor did he read 1 Timothy 5:17, which says, "Elders who do their work well should be respected and paid well, especially those who work hard at both preaching and teaching. For the Scripture says, 'You must not muzzle an ox to keep it from eating as it treads out the grain.' And in another place, 'Those who work deserve their pay!'" (NLT); also, I already knew that the man didn't know Galatians 6:6, which says, "Those who are taught the word of God should provide for their teachers, sharing all good things with them" (NLT). I knew this man was ignorant of what the Word of God says regarding paying those who serve in the ministry so that they can continue to focus on doing the work of the ministry, but so are many people in and out of the church; so I took a few minutes to explain to him the basic expenses of the ministry: the power bill, the gas bill, the cost of television broadcasts, the cost of outreach work; I explained to him that the ones who go into the strip clubs to minister to strippers, the ones who walk the streets rescuing girls and boys from the human sex-trafficking industry and from prostitution; and the ones who perform outreach to the poor and needy, providing them with free haircuts, showers, clothes, food, free job training classes and computer literacy skills so that they can get a job, free drug and alcohol rehabilitation services, shelter, etc., they are only able to do what they do based on the giving of the members of the congregations where they serve. So, the next time he felt like complaining about giving, I reminded him to think about the cost of ministry...and then I reminded him of why an effective pastor is worth their salary, especially if that pastor has singlehandedly taken their ministry from being a storefront church with only five members to a mega-ministry with both national and international ministries and outreach programs operating on a million dollar budget. (I reminded him that the night club he was getting ready to go to that night was going to charge him for every little thing, from entrance into the club to the drinks, and that no one at that club was going to share with him the Word of God, which is able to save his soul, change his life, transform his character, restore his broken relationships, break the strongholds of addiction and emotional and psychological bondages off of his life, provide aid and assistance to both he and his family when in need, nor was the bartender going to take the time to listen to any of his problems, which are just a few of the things the ministries he vehemently criticized do on a daily basis.) After I was done explaining all of this to him, he had no rebuttal. Some people just need to see all that it takes to effectively do ministry just so that they can see a small portion of the cost that is required.

When the Apostle Peter spoke about ministry in the book of Acts chapter 6, verse 3, he called it a "business". I find it important to stress to people that ministry is just that: a business. Like a business, it takes capital to run, it requires workers, it must market itself in order to remain visible, and it must always take advantage of the latest technologies if it is going to avoid falling into the abyss of irrelevance in a constantly changing and progressing society. The message of the church is timeless and should never change, but the means by which it communicates and promotes its message are and must constantly be changing. For example, the majority of the youth today spend a great deal of their time on social media, browsing the web on their cell phones, watching Youtube and Facebook Live and other apps. Churches that refuse to embrace the latest vehicles of communication may end up looking like the ghost towns of America, which are merely landmarks highlighting the shifts and transitions in cultural trends. These were towns that once had booming economies due to their proximity to railroads but have since become irrelevant due to the fact that Americans no longer rely on railroads as a primary means of transportation after the emergence of cars and airplanes, which have changed the dynamics of America's social and economic landscape. The churches that want to hold on to archaic means of communication today are delusional; they prefer dial-up internet as opposed to Comcast high-speed internet; they prefer horse-and-buggies as opposed to today's high-powered vehicles that will leave horses laying in the dust. I hate to admit this, but the kingdom of Satan tends to remain on the cutting edge while many of God's people cling onto the old ways, gloating over the acquisition of the wheel while the devil's emissaries gloat over the acquisition of anti-gravity propulsion systems.

Satan spends more money than the church to get his message out to the masses and this is precisely why all of the mainstream media, Hollywood, and even academia is filled with content promoting nothing but antichrist, anti-Christian messages. This is one of the biggest reasons secularism, humanism, feminism, liberalism, occultism, and every other ideology that's antithetical of Christ's gospel is dominating western society today and is beginning to slowly push Christianity out of the public sphere. Satan is willing to take the risk and make the financial investment to get his message out, realizing that he will see the results of his financial sacrifice. Unfortunately, many Christians don't seem to see the big picture. While we tightly grip our wallets and purses due to the reluctance to let go and give financially—and when we finally do give, it's usually a small amount—Satan has his emissaries and followers giving big bucks to advance his kingdom in the earth.

If one of the most important signs of the end-times is the preaching of the gospel all over the globe according to Matthew 24:14, which says,

> "And this gospel of the kingdom shall be preached in all the world for a witness unto all nations; and then shall the end come..."

then this reveals to us one of the main reasons Christ hasn't returned to establish His throne on the earth: Christ is waiting for the church to finish its evangelistic work in the earth.

The gospel must reach every corner of the globe. 2 Peter 3:9 says, "The Lord isn't really being slow about his promise, as some people think. No, he is being patient for your sake. He does not want anyone to be destroyed, but wants everyone to repent" (NLT). God is simply giving men time to respond to the gospel and repent, but how can anyone respond to the gospel message and repent of their sins unless a preacher preaches it to them; and furthermore, how can that preacher reach them with the gospel unless they be sent (Romans 10:15); and in order to send the preacher with his or her team and resources, this takes . . . You got it: money!

When the Apostle Paul wrote, "But my God shall supply all your need according to his riches in glory by Christ Jesus" in Philippians 4:19, in context he was speaking to the Church of Macedonia who had supplied him with the finances to carry out his missionary journey; for Paul, in the verse prior, wrote, "I have all I need and more, now that I have received your gifts from Epaphroditus. They are a sweet smelling aroma, an acceptable sacrifice, well-pleasing to God" (vs. 18). Paul told this group of Believers that their financial offering, which they gave him to help him continue the work of evangelism, was a "sweet smelling" fragrance in God's nostrils, one that God saw as a pleasing sacrifice to Himself. Paul assured these people that because they went out of their way to ensure that he was supplied with everything he needed to continue preaching the gospel, God was going to go out of His way to meet their every need. When one reads this verse, it is important that they understand the context in which it is written: God repays those who go out of their way to finance the preaching of the gospel. Yes! You are doing God a favor by financing the gospel, and He, in return, will do you a favor. Paul mentioned the same thing to the church of Corinth while explaining to them about the importance of sowing financially into the ministry:

> "For God is the one who provides seed for the farmer and then bread to eat. In the same way, he will provide and increase your resources and then produce a great harvest of generosity in you. Yes, you will be enriched in every way so that you can always be generous. And when we take your gifts to those who need them, they will thank God. So two good things will result from this ministry of giving—the needs of the believers in Jerusalem will be met, and they will joyfully express their thanks to God." (2 Corinthians 9:10-12, NLT)

Your money is your seed. Eat it. Throw it away. Or sow it. It's totally up to you. If you give it to God by financing His evangelistic work, you'll cause it to become a seed that produce a harvest of blessings from God's own hand in return. This is why seed sowing is so important. If you help God accomplish His goals in the earth, He will remember what you did for Him and pay you back. If you don't care about what's important to God, then why should He care about what's important to you? That's fair. It's that simple.

CHAPTER TWO

The Truth About Seed Faith

MY JOURNEY TOWARDS THE REVELATION OF financial sowing and reaping is no different than anyone else's. No, an angel didn't descend gracefully from the heavens with a golden chalice in its hands filled with divine revelation and then pour it into my head. Mine is quite simple: I had to go to church and listen to a preacher and then make the decision to act on the information I had just been given. As I further researched the matter, I learned that for years I had been robbed of vital information needed for my success in the Christian faith. I'd skimmed the Bible and come across a few verses talking about *seed faith*, but the revelation of seed faith had not yet sunk in, not until the pastor of our church began to really teach on it.

I must stop here and give credit where credit is due.

I learned about seed faith from my pastor and father, Rev. Timothy Flemming, Sr. But where did he learn it from? He didn't grow up with the revelation of seed faith either. My dad came up in a very traditional religious setting. Growing up in the Primitive Baptist Church in middle Georgia, there wasn't much talk, if any, about seed faith, about sowing financially and reaping a financial harvest, about turning our money into a seed. When people usually talked about sowing and reaping, it was in the context of our actions: *If you sow kindness, you'll reap kindness; etc.* And this is true. Jesus said in John 6:38, "Give, and it will be given to you. A good measure, pressed down, shaken together and running over, will be poured into your lap. For with the measure you use, it will be measured to you." In context, this verse refers to the giving of mercy and forgiveness, not the giving of money; but it still carries the logic of sowing and reaping, and more specifically, the implication that you only reap that which you sow and that a seed can only reproduce after its own kind. The same logic behind John 6:38 applies to the area of finances: you reap *what* you sow. Many people assume money plays by its own set of rules. In past generations, whenever Believers talked about wealth, they usually assumed that the only way to acquire it was to get a college degree (although, in rural Georgia that wasn't actually a deal-breaker at that time either) so that you can get a high-paying job or you had to be the recipient of passed-down money (a big inheritance). Few sermons, if any, dealt with God's Kingdom principles regarding financial prosperity; they only focused on the natural means of doing things while disregarding the supernatural way of doing things. God desires to be the one who provides supernaturally for us so that only He gets the glory and so that other people may begin to inquire of Him after witnessing Him at work in our lives (Zechariah 4:6).

My dad came into the knowledge of seed faith after God radically transformed our church. It happened so suddenly. One Sunday morning, God's anointing invaded our traditional Baptist church and turned it upside down. We went from strict traditions that forbade the charismatic gifts of the Holy Spirit to now operating in the gift of tongues, the word of knowledge, prophecy, laying on of hands, etc. We began to get in line with the teachings of the Bible. We cut out dues and fundraisers and began to strictly focus on tithing. But God wasn't done yet. In the upcoming days, God connected our ministry with anointed men and women of faith who understood the principle of seed faith; Evangelist Benny Hinn was one of those individuals. My dad began to grow more and more interested in the anointing, which is what caused him to seek out Evangelist Hinn. While attending Evangelist Hinn's crusades, he began to hear about seed faith and be challenged in that area. Now armed with this information, my dad began teaching it to his congregation. Instantly, our church saw rapid growth in its finances, and this financial growth came even as the church lost members due to some individuals not being able to embrace certain changes. We experienced a financial breakthrough as a result of following the principles of tithing and seed sowing.

WHAT IS A SEED OFFERING AND WHAT DIFFERENTIATES IT FROM A TITHE?

A seed offering and a tithe are two totally different things. A seed is an offering you give voluntarily, out of love for God and the ministry; but a tithe is not a voluntary thing; it is an offering that we owe to God as part of our covenant condition. A seed is something you plant with the expectation that it will reproduce itself and grow into a harvest. A tithe is more like a tax—and you don't sow taxes; you pay them.

In Malachi 3:8-9, God asked,

> "Will a mere mortal rob God? Yet you rob me. 'But you ask, 'How are we robbing you?' 'In tithes and offerings. You are under a curse—your whole nation—because you are robbing me." (NIV)

Notice God's sharp rebuke here and the language He uses when speaking of the tithe. God considers the tithe to belong to Him solely. God has placed a demand on the tithe, revealing that it's not optional. Tithing is a must. Now, the debate among some scholars is whether or not the law of the tithe should rest under the category of God's moral laws or the ceremonial laws of the Old Testament, which are no longer applicable in a physical sense today. (There are 613 Old Testament laws in the Torah, and they are divided into three categories: the moral laws, the ceremonial laws, and the civil laws. The moral laws are timeless and immutable, never changing. They still apply to us today. Grace doesn't cancel our obligation to hold on to God's moral commandments such as not stealing, not committing murder, not lying, not coveting our neighbors' belongings, not worshiping idols, honoring our parents, etc. These commandments are reiterated in the New Testament in the writings of Paul, Peter, James, John and the other writers, and Jesus also tells us to observe them if we are to establish a relationship with Him in John 15:7-15.) The reality is, as I explained earlier in the introduction, the commandment to tithe is not relegated to the Old Testament Levitical system to begin with; it predates the laws of Moses being that it was a practice that was already in use centuries before Moses by Abraham and his descendants. The tithe is one of those timeless, immutable practices just like the moral laws; therefore, we're to always honor God with our increase by giving to Him the first and best portion of it. We can't negotiate with God on this. That money is His alone. In fact, the literal meaning of the word "tithe" is "a tenth." So, all God requires of us is that we give Him one-tenth of our increase, which, in our case, would be one-tenth of our gross income, not our net income.

I've been asked before if we must tithe from our federal income tax checks at the beginning of the year. If we've been tithing from our gross all year long, then no, we don't have to tithe out of our federal income tax money because we've been tithing out of that money all year long. The one thing you can do is sow a seed out of that income tax money.

The tithe was to be brought into the "storehouse of

the Lord" according to Malachi 3:10, which was a designated place or "the place God chose to place His name on," which is reiterated in Deuteronomy 14:22: "the designated place". When reading Malachi chapter three, it is noteworthy to mention that God was specifically addressing the Levitical priests who were responsible for collecting the tithes from the Israelites first and then bringing one-tenth of that which they had collected into the temple for God's "storehouse" as revealed in Nehemiah 10:37–38. Out of all of the tithes collected, only 1% made it to the temple; the rest went to the Levitical cities to be kept and used by the Levites. So, when God spoke of those who were robbing Him, He was talking about the Levites; but we must keep in mind that all of Israel was required by God to tithe. God said the Levites and "even this whole nation" was robbing Him.

The tithe was to go not only to the appropriate place, but it was to fall into the appropriate hands also. In the book of Acts, you will notice it wasn't the members taking up the offering; it was the Apostles taking up the offering (Acts 5). In the temple, it wasn't the people taking up the offering; it was the Levites. Later on, we see Jesus taking up the offering in the temple in Luke 21:1-4. Whether it be the church, the temple, or the synagogue, God has always held the clerical leadership responsible for handling the offerings. This order was never abandoned. God's house still operates off of the principle of a *designated place* and *designated hands* handling God's offerings. Today, the place God has chosen to place His name on is the church, and the clerical leadership would be the apostles, pastor, elders, the deacons, etc.: the leadership of the church (1 Timothy chapter three; Titus 1:5; Acts 15:4; Ephesians 4:11; etc.). As Paul established different churches in different cities, he placed elders over these churches. In Acts 20:28, the word "elder" is translated **επισκοπους** (episkopous) and it means "overseer". Each separate church had its own overseer (or bishop as its translated in some places). These overseers were responsible for the administration of the church; this entailed the handling of its finances. The early church was very well structured.

Some people argue in opposition of tithing based on the possibility that those receiving the tithes might abuse them—use them for the wrong purposes. Well, ironically, those same individuals never argue against paying taxes to Uncle Sam based off of the obvious misuse of tax dollars by bureaucrats in Washington, nor do they complain about the use of funds by banks, colleges and universities, non-profit organizations and other entities that have been trusted with handling money. God actually recognizes every giver and blesses them for their obedience to His ordinances and He promises not to hold them accountable for the wrongdoings of those individuals He placed in positions of authority as explained in Colosians 3:23-25 and Ezekiel chapter 18.

The big question is did the early church fathers talk about tithing? Did they believe in tithing? Yes. Perhaps, the most prominant early church leader, the Apostle Paul, discussed tithing in 1 Corinthians 9:13-14 where he wrote, "Do ye not know that they which minister about holy things live of the things of the temple? and they which wait at the altar are partakers with the altar? Even so hath the Lord ordained that they which preach the gospel should live of the gospel." The Apostle Paul, while defending his authority as an apostle, engaged in what theologians call parallelism, which is where he used an Old Testament principle to explain how the church is supposed to operate. There, Paul cites the Old Testament model—how the Levites were supported by the tithes—which is established in the law of Moses as the model God "ordered" for the church today. But Paul wasn't the only one advocating for the tithe in the early church:

> "The Jews were constrained to a regular payment of Tithes; Christians who have liberty assign all their possessions to the Lord bestowing freely not the lesser portions of their property since they have the hope of greater things."— Irenaeus (130-202 AD)

According to Irenaeus, Christians should not only commit to paying the tithe (tenth), but should even give above that. To Irenaeus, the tithe should be the minimum amount that's required because of the higher standard God holds Believers to.

> "Woe to him, it is said, who doeth not alms; and if this was the case under the Old Covenant, much more is it under the New. If, where the getting of wealth was allowed and the enjoyment of it, and

> the care of it, there was such provision made for the succoring of the poor, how much more in that Dispensation, where we are commanded to surrender all we have? For what did not they of old do?"—John Chrysostom (349–407 AD)

So, according to John Chrysostom, the Archbishop of Constantinople, the Law of Christ actually supercedes the Law of Moses. Under the Law of Moses, for example, engaging in the physical act of sex outside of marriage was considered adultery; but under the Law of Christ, merely lusting in one's heart after someone who is not yours is considered adultery. Under this rule, therefore, the Law of Moses is not iradicated, but rather, it is ampliphied and made a mater of both the heart as well as the body. Plainly put: If tithing was a requirement under Moses' Law, it's more of a requirement under Christ's Law.

Chrysostom also stated,

> "They gave tithes, and tithes again upon tithes for orphans, widows, and strangers, whereas someone was saying to me in astonishment at another, 'Why, such an one givest tithes.' What a load of disgrace does this expression imply, since what was not a matter of wonder with the Jews has come to be so in the case of the Christians? If there was danger then in omitting tithes, think how great it must be now."

Chrysostom admonished the Believers who asked, "Why... givest tithes?" calling their attitude a "load of disgrace." He also iterated that if non-tithing was something that got us in trouble under the Law of Moses in the Old Testament, then the penalty for not tithing is even greater under the Law of Christ today.

Now, a seed is optional according to Scripture. Seed offerings are not obligatory or mandatory. With regards to the seed, this is your opportunity to choose whether or not you want to be blessed beyond that of the norm. Your tithe can't be your seed because that money belongs to God, but your seed is yours to give and control. You won't be cursed by God for holding on to a seed like you would for holding on to the tithe. Oftentimes, ministers abusing the principle of the seed offering will cite Acts 5:1-11, which records the story of Ananias and Sapphira, the two individuals that died during the offering time. Some ministers will claim that the two were killed by God because they would not participate in a mandatory offering. First of all, the offering that Peter and the apostles were taking up wasn't a mandatory offering since everyone had a choice whether or not to give. Secondly, Ananias and Sapphira were cursed by God not because they didn't give—for the text makes it obvious that they gave—but for another reason. The reason God cursed them is found in verses three and four, which reads:

> "Then Peter said, 'Ananias, why have you let Satan fill your heart? You lied to the Holy Spirit, and you

> kept some of the money for yourself. The property was yours to sell or not sell, as you wished. And after selling it, the money was also yours to give away. How could you do a thing like this? You weren't lying to us but to God!'" (NLT)

Ananias and his wife, Sapphira, died not because they didn't give that day, but because they lied to the Holy Spirit about how much they were giving. Peter reminded them that their money was theirs to do what they wanted with, but testing God by lying to Him—as if He couldn't see what they were trying to do—was a different situation altogether. Ananias and Sapphira were trying to manipulate God through lying just so that they could get acknowledged publicly before the church just as Barnabas had been. That's what got them in trouble. According to Jesus, giving simply to be seen is still prohibited by God (Matthew 6:2-4).

The seed is money you give above your tithe, out of your own free will and love for God. The seed sets us up to receive blessings above and beyond that of the ordinary. In Scripture, whenever the seed is mentioned, we also find that this is the only offering where we can determine the actual measure that we'll receive in return. The tithe is set, but not the seed. In essence, when it comes to the seed, it's as if God is asking you, "How big do you want your blessing to be?"

Another interesting difference between the seed and the tithe is this: the tithe doesn't produce a harvest; it simply guarantees God's protection over your harvest. As Malachi

3:10-11 states,

> "'Bring the whole tithe into the storehouse, that there may be food in my house. Test me in this,' says the LORD Almighty, 'and see if I will not throw open the floodgates of heaven and pour out so much blessing that there will not be room enough to store it. I will prevent pests from devouring your crops, and the vines in your fields will not drop their fruit before it is ripe,' says the LORD Almighty.'" (NIV)

Notice here that the promise of God was and is to pour out "a blessing" (favor) upon the people by causing their crops to grow and not be eaten up by insects that usually feed on crops in a field (locusts, canker worms, etc.). You don't need a pesticide when God's hand is protecting your crops. But not only was that God's promise to the Israelites; God also said He would prevent their vines from dropping their fruit before the fruit was ripe, which meant that God would see to it that their crops flourished and blossomed as opposed to growing partially and falling before the perfect time. So, in that sense, God's promise to us is that our tithes will cause Him to preserve and prosper the seeds that we sow into His Kingdom by sending down the rain that they need to grow (which is implied by the "windows of heaven". This phrase was often associated with rain since rain comes from the sky above. The ancients would seek to appease their gods for the purpose of receiving rain for their crops, knowing that if there was no rain then they wouldn't grow any crops and would therefore starve to death). And not only will God ensure that your crops grow, but He'll protect them from the many troubles waiting to devour them once they come. Some people don't realize that it is a miracle that their income hasn't been eaten up by things like unexpected medical bills, sudden expenses, and sudden troubles. They don't realize that their income is actually being protected by God as a result of their honoring Him with their tithes. Lastly, God will prevent your vine from casting its fruit before the right time or moment. This is so significant, especially for those who are big dreamers and are looking to accomplish big things in life. Timing is everything. In business, it's very important that you don't pitch the right idea at the wrong time. For individuals who invest in stocks and bonds, they understand the importance of timing better than anyone. Entrepreneurs know the importance of timing and location also. For example, some start-up companies have started at the right time and some at the wrong time. Some companies began at a time when the technology needed to sustain them was widely used or available to the public. Imagine if Youtube had have come out in the early 1990's. They would not have succeeded because the technology that is needed to watch videos on computers wasn't available to all. People would have needed too many plug-ins and would've grown weary of trying to download and watch them; also, internet speed times were significantly lower, which would have also been a source of frustration and a cause of exhaustion for consumers. By Youtube coming into being when it did, it was able to flourish because the conditions were ripe. It can't be overstated the importance of timing when it comes to everything we do. God promises that He will ensure that your heart's desires and plans will flourish at the right time.

MISCONCEPTIONS ABOUT SEED FAITH

Now, if you were to spend a little time researching the subject of seed faith you are bound to discover countless articles and blogs decrying it as a church scam or a form of heresy or error. And to be honest, that's to be expected. There are a number of legitimate biblical practices that are considered unbiblical and heretical by certain Believers. For example, many churches today simply do not believe in the anointing of the Holy Spirit, neither do they believe in the charismatic gifts of the Holy Spirit that are talked about in the book of 1 Corinthians. When our church first received the anointing and began to embrace the power of God and the gifts of the Spirit, there were some churches that began to separate from us, fearing that we had fallen into heresy. How dare we speak in tongues! Certain pastors, fearful of change, began to back away from us, not wanting to be associated with something they'd been taught to believe was of Satan. For the most part, I've discovered that many people simply don't embrace what the Bible says over what their denomination and its leaders say. That's a big problem.

A survey conducted by LifeWay Research for Ligonier Ministries found some interesting statistics regarding what many Evangelical Christians today believe about God and salvation. In an article entitled *New Poll Finds Evangelicals' Favorite Heresies* published on ChristianityToday.com, it is revealed that 22% of Evangelicals believe Jesus is "less divine than the Heavenly Father" (that's nearly a quarter of the Evangelical community), and more that 51% of Evangelicals believe the Holy Spirit isn't even a person, but that He's a force or energy, which is actually in alignment with New Age philosophy rather than the Bible. So, with over half of the Evangelical community not even believing in the literal person of the Holy Spirit, it's no wonder so many call the anointing and the gifts of the Spirit witchcraft and mysticism. Well, that makes the Apostle Paul one of the biggest witches and mystics on the planet since he operated regularly in signs and wonders through the anointing of the Holy Spirit. That would also fall in line with the train of thought of the Pharisees who lambasted Jesus as having performed miracles through the power of Beelzebub in Matthew 12:24-27, to which Jesus responded that Satan cannot cast out Satan, implying that there exist two powers in the universe that are at war with one another and that not all displays of supernaturalism are from Satan and not all displays of supernaturalism are from God—you must have the discernment of the Holy Spirit to know which "power" is at work in any given situation (1 John 4:1). *But hey, if you don't even believe in the Holy Spirit, how are you even going to rely on the Holy Spirit for that discernment?*

Now, regarding seed faith, we are looking at a similar situation: people who are denominationally bound or are misled by wrong interpretations of Scripture are fighting against something that is repeatedly being taught and demonstrated in the Bible. The Apostle Paul talked extensively about seed faith in his letters to the churches. One thing I need to inject here is that the Apostle Paul operated in a realm of divine revelation that not even the other apostles operated in as acknowledged even by Peter who wrote, "And remember, our Lord's patience gives people time to be saved. This is what our beloved brother Paul also wrote to you with *the wisdom God gave him*—speaking of these things in all of his letters. *Some of his comments are hard to understand*, and those who are ignorant and unstable have twisted his letters to mean something quite different, just as they do with other parts of Scripture. And this will result in their destruction" (1 Peter 3:15-16, NLT). Paul explained in Galatians 1:11-18 that many of the revelations he received were not given to him by Peter and the other apostles, but rather, he received them directly from God Himself while camping out in Arabia for three years, spending time with no one but God in prayer. So Paul received revelations that even Peter admitted were "hard to understand" (or much more profound and in-depth than his). With that being said, most of our understanding of seed faith comes from the revelations of the Apostle Paul and the Old Testament—but so does most of our revelation on the grace of God come from Paul. It was Paul who urged Christians to sow financially in Philippians and 2 Corinthians with the promise that God would bless them in return for their sacrifices. In Philippians 4:19, Paul was specifically speaking of God blessing the Macedonian Believers due to their financial sacrifices; and in 2 Corinthians chapter nine, Paul was speaking specifically about money as a seed, not other acts of service. Yes, we all realize that there are many different seeds we can give, but in those two passages of Scripture money was the topic.

Now, I understand where a lot of the anger comes from whenever people speak about seed faith. Yes, there are people who have abused this principle and have taken it to the extreme, even to the point of throwing out false promises to people, which God never endorsed. In reality, there will always be false prophets around. We can't rid the world of them. God will one day. But for now, we just have to be discerning and know God's Word enough to be able to "divide the truth" (2 Timothy 2:15). With that being said, I'll address the elephant in the room: the prosperity gospel. There is no such thing as a "prosperity gospel". The gospel is not about getting money. Yes, that's a heretical doctrine. In fact, in 2 Timothy chapter six, Paul exposed that heresy. Paul wrote,

> "Anyone who teaches something different is arrogant and lacks understanding. Such a person has an unhealthy desire to quibble over the meaning of words. This stirs up arguments ending in jealousy, division, slander, and evil suspicions. These people always cause trouble. Their minds are corrupt, and

> they have turned their backs on the truth. *To them, a show of godliness is just a way to become wealthy.* Yet true godliness with contentment is itself great wealth. After all, we brought nothing with us when we came into the world, and we can't take anything with us when we leave it. So if we have enough food and clothing, let us be content. *But people who long to be rich fall into temptation and are trapped by many foolish and harmful desires that plunge them into ruin and destruction. For the love of money is the root of all kinds of evil. And some people, craving money, have wandered from the true faith and pierced themselves with many sorrows.*" (1 Timothy 6:5-10, NLT)

Regarding ministers looking to get rich off of spiritual gifts and the anointing, there is a judgment awaiting them, and God will expose their false motives. Actually, all you have to do is watch their actions. You'll discover that the love of money will cause them to veer off of the path of the gospel and cause them to compromise their faith for financial gain and advantageous positions. Sadly, the longer they continue in the wrong spirit, the wider that chasm will grow between them and the pure gospel message. But it is noteworthy to mention that the same Paul who condemned the love of money and materialism and stressed to us the need for contentment in every circumstance is the same Paul who had no qualms with asking for money from his churches to finance the needs of the hurting Christians in Jerusalem and to finance his own missionary journeys. Paul revealed the purpose for the money he was requesting, emphasizing that it wasn't to be spent on himself for his own selfish reasons, but he wasn't afraid to ask, knowing money was a necessity. We must remember that this is the same Apostle Paul also who explained in 1 Corinthians chapter nine that ministers should get paid for what they do so that they can continue to do the work of ministry without worrying about how they're going to provide for themselves and their families. So, while Paul criticized the greed of false teachers on the one hand, he also criticized the stinginess of Christians who were reluctant to give to the Kingdom. He stated in Philippians 4:15, "As you know, you Philippians were the only ones who gave me financial help when I first brought you the Good News and then traveled on from Macedonia. No other church did this" (NLT). Paul's disappointment with the other churches was apparent. He was upset that no other church cared enough about his needs as a minister to sow into him FINANCIALLY. Paul admonished the church of Corinth, in essence shaming them for not stepping up to the plate like the Macedonian Christians. He wrote,

> "Now I want you to know, dear brothers and sisters, *what God in his kindness has done through the churches in Macedonia*. They are being tested by many troubles, and they are very poor. But they are also filled with abundant joy, which has overflowed in rich generosity. For I can testify that they gave not only what

> they could afford, but far more. And they did it of their own free will. *They begged us again and again for the privilege of sharing in the gift for the believers in Jerusalem.* They even did more than we had hoped, for their first action was to give themselves to the Lord and to us, just as God wanted them to do. *So we have urged Titus, who encouraged your giving in the first place, to return to you and encourage you to finish this ministry of giving. Since you excel in so many ways—in your faith, your gifted speakers, your knowledge, your enthusiasm, and your love from us—I want you to excel also in this gracious act of giving.* I am not commanding you to do this. *But I am testing how genuine your love is by comparing it with the eagerness of the other churches.*" (2 Corinthians 8:1-8, NLT)

Ouch! What a rebuke! Paul, in essence, told the church of Corinth to put their money where their mouths were—to not only talk about how much they loved God, but prove it the same way the Macedonian Christians did. Paul said he was "testing how genuine" their "love" was by challenging them in the area of giving. This goes back to what we covered in chapter one. Furthermore, this shows how grieved Paul was with Christians who were too stingy to give but wanted to receive so much from God. In the King James version, Paul's challenge is worded this way: "I speak not by commandment, but by occasion of the forwardness of others, and to prove the sincerity of your love" (2 Corinthians 8:8). In other words, Paul was saying, *I'm here to give you the opportunity to prove you actually love God by giving to the Kingdom financially*. Paul said you can excel in everything else—faith, good preaching, your theological understanding, etc.—but if you can't excel in the area of financial giving, then you don't love God the way you profess to. Financial giving is a real test, a sacrifice that proves the sincerity of your faith and love for God. You NEED money and can't effectively manage without it. What are the odds that God tests us with the one thing we need perhaps more than anything else in this world to live?

Biblical seed faith is not about getting rich; it's about financing Kingdom work. Seed faith is not about purchasing blessings from God because you can't—when one man tried to purchase the anointing of God, Peter cursed him for thinking he could do so (Acts 8:18-20). But when God sees that you're willing to give Him what you need the most just to finance His agenda in the earth, He will honor your giving with a blessing. That's why Paul said don't give out of necessity or coercion, but give like the Macedonians did: out of the joy in your heart; with great eagerness because of your love for God, His Word, and His people that is in your heart. Paul noted that a person who gives with this type of excitement and joy actually gains the attention of God and warms His heart (2 Corinthians 9:7). Keep this in mind: you are not cursed by God because you didn't sow a seed; you'll be cursed if you withhold God's tithes (Malachi 3:9; Mark 12:17). So, don't let any fool you into thinking that you are cursed by God because you didn't give a seed offering. This is a trick of the enemy. Paul said we're to never give grudgingly nor out of necessity—basically, don't give unwillingly and reluctantly nor give because you feel obligated due to outside pressure. Such giving is a violation of Scripture.

Whenever you give an offering based on the wrong principles, you're not sowing money, you're actually throwing away your money. The thing that transforms your money into a seed is when the giving is done not out of force and coercion, but out of love for God and the things of God. In essences, your attitude transforms your money into a seed (I'll cover this in more detail in a later chapter).

Yes, there is a component of seed faith that promises that when we give to the Kingdom of God, He will bless us in return. God can't be bought, but He can be moved by our willingness to give our best and even our last and trust Him (Mark 12:41-44); and furthermore, we can see time and time again that when an individual sows in obedience to God, He blesses them tremendously. Such was the promise made to the rich young ruler in Luke 18:28-30, where Jesus promised us this: "'Yes,' Jesus replied, 'and I assure you that everyone who has given up house or wife or brothers or parents or children, for the sake of the Kingdom of God, *will be repaid many times over in this life*, and will have eternal life in the world to come'" (NLT). God dispenses blessings as a result of our sowing based on two things: His love for givers and His promise made to givers. God blesses us out of appreciation for our giving, but He also blesses us out of a principle He established, that principle being: You reap what you sow, especially when it comes to finances (Proverbs 11:25; Psalm 41:1; Proverbs 19:17; Matthew 6:19-21; Matthew 10:42; Deuteronomy 15:10; Deuteronomy 16:17; Matthew 6:3-4; 2 Corinthians 9:6-8; 1 Corinthians 16:2; etc.). Each of these verses listed contains this language: If you give to that which God instructs you to give, you'll receive a blessing in return. That is an established principle that you should put into practice. Remember: If giving to the poor sets you up to reap a blessing from God, how much more will giving to the Kingdom of God and the work of ministry set you up to reap a mighty blessing from God (Galatians 6:9-10)? Paul used the word "reap" when speaking of the blessings that come back to us. This speaks of an established law. The ground doesn't give back to us because it likes us; it gives back to us when we sow into it because it is governed by a natural law that God put in motion. The same is to be said about financial sowing and reaping.

In Acts 4:31-37, one of the side-effects of the Holy Spirit's presence in the church in Jerusalem was that Believers began to sell land and bring their money to the apostles so that they could distribute financial aid to those in need. When God's presence enters into the room greed is obliterated, not sustained. When God's presence enters a person's life, that person actually becomes more willing to give, not more reluctant to give. Seed faith is based on the Holy Spirit's prodding, His guidance; it is also based on our love for God and the things of God. Yes, we should sow with the expectation to reap, understanding that reaping is based on the fact that God desires for us to reap so that we will have more to sow into His Kingdom agenda.

MY FIRST EXPERIMENT WITH SEED FAITH

I was 16 years old when I first experimented with seed faith. My mind had been challenged now. I knew what tithing was and was now discovering what sowing seed into the Kingdom of God was. I began to see clearly that you must give in order to receive, but now it was time to put it into action.

During this time, I was a junior in high school. I'd been blessed to get my first car. It was a red Toyota Tercel hash-back, 1982 model. It lacked many things: air conditioning, a radio, and a few minor luxuries, but it worked—it drove; it got me from point A to point B. To me, that's what mattered the most at that time. At that time, I knew someone who was struggling badly. He was in college and was working a job to support himself. His car had just broken down on him, leaving him without transportation. It was at that moment that I felt God leading me to sow my car into that individual, which I did. I went to that person and told him I was signing the title deed over to him and giving him the keys to my car free of charge. He was very appreciative. After that, I went back to riding the school bus and catching rides with others whenever available to get around.

A few days passed after I sowed that car into the life of someone else. It was now my birthday. I was excited, and even more excited over the fact that I had been blessed with a hundred dollars as a gift. With that hundred dollars in my hand I began to think of several things I wanted to do with it...that is, until the Holy Spirit whispered into my heart to sow all of it in church one Sunday while the pastor was appealing to the congregation to sow a hundred dollar seed. So, what did I do? I got up and sowed that hundred dollars into the offering that morning. I sowed my car and all of my cash in two weeks time. My mother, perhaps, didn't understand the significance of her words when she declared that Sunday morning after I sowed that financial seed, "God is getting ready to blessed you mightily." Not even she was prepared for the blessing God was getting ready to bestow upon my life at that time.

In the days following, my dad came to me and said He wanted to get me another car so that I could get around on my own. At the time, he had a budget of only $4,000 to spend on a vehicle. We got out and drove around from one car lot to another just looking to find a good used car within that budget. We couldn't find anything. For at least two days we looked only to come up empty-handed. If the car was decent, it was too much. If the car was within my dad's budget, it wasn't decent. It was frustrating. But later that week, a friend scooped by to pick me up to run an errand. We were driving down a back road when, all of a sudden, we spotted the most beautiful car parked in a plot of land right across from a gas station. It was for sale for $4,800. We jotted down the number on the for sale sign and then rushed back to the house to inform my dad that we had found "the one". Me, my dad, and my friend then drove back to that spot to take a closer look at the car. It was a red Mazda RX7, 1987 model that was in mint condition. The man working at the gas station across the street informed us that people had been stopping buy to inquire about that car every day since it has been out there, but for some reason no one could seem to buy it. Then he uttered these words without fully knowing what was coming out of his mouth: "It's as if this car has been sitting there waiting for you." We called the car's seller and he came out to meet us. It was an old Caucasian man; a kind and gentle-hearted individual dressed in overalls. He certainly didn't look like the sports car type. He explained to us why he was selling the car in the first place. He said he originally had the car for his grandson who lived with him, but his grandson didn't want to do right by him and do right in school. As punishment, he took the car away with the promise of giving it back only if the boy behaved, but the grandson decided to continue misbehaving, thereby prompting the old man to put the car up for sale.

The car had less than 20,000 miles on it. When it cranked up the engine roared like a lion. When I cut the air conditioning on, frost blew out—it was that cold. When I turned the radio on music played—it actually had working speakers that sounded good. When I hit the nitro button the car accelerated instantly. Everything was practically brand new as if the car had barely been driven. YES!! And the car's seller agreed to drop the selling price down to . . . $4,000. That day, I drove off of that lot with practically a brand new sports car. When I arrived home, my mom was shocked that I ended up with such a fancy car. She'd forgotten the words that she declared just a few days prior.

Let's unpack this. First, God challenged me to sow, and I obeyed. He challenged me to give my all, which I did. Secondly, God began to work behind the scenes to cause the circumstances to line up in my favor: a hard-headed grandson lost a jewel of a car; my dad's finances wouldn't permit him to spend above a certain amount, thereby eliminating all of the decent cars being presented at the car lots; a friend stops by suddenly on a certain day and we have to run a certain errand, one that puts us on a back road we hardly ever travel, which is where we found the perfect car at the perfect price in the perfect condition waiting just for me. Is this a coincidence? Of course not! Each and every incident was divinely orchestrated by God.

God had me to sow that which was precious to me at the time in order to receive the best He had for me. If I had gotten hung up on that little Toyota Tercel (with no AC and no radio), unwilling to let it go due to some extreme attachment, anxiety, and fear of lost, I wouldn't have ended up with a sports car that dwarfed what I previously had. Whenever God challenges you to give up something, it's because He always has something better in mind. If you let go of what God tells you to let go of when He tells you to let go of it, you will discover that what you're releasing doesn't even compare to what God has in store for you due to your obedience.

In the years to come, I would discover that God always supplies us with THE BEST whenever we obey Him in the area of seed sowing. God would issue several more challenges, all of which produced mind-blowing miracles and blessings in my life. It all started with a seed. It all started with a challenge to sow given to me by the Holy Spirit.

Chapter Three

To Sow... Or Not To Sow?

During my freshman year in high school, I developed a sudden interest in poetry. Now, I have always been creative in the arts. I loved drawing and even creating my own comic books when I was a child. But I had never written a poem until my ninth grade in high school. Prior to this, my aspiration was to be an athlete. I spent more time on the football field and in the boxing ring than anything else. But now, God was redirecting my passion in another direction.

By the time I reached my junior year, I had completely given up sports and began focusing full-time in the area of creative writing. I became the editor of my school's literary magazine, which I remained both my junior and senior year. I was immersed in a world of poetry and short stories, both writing them and editing them for our school's magazine. I then began studying other great poets like Emily Dickinson, Langston Hughes, Paul Lawrence Dunbar, and more. Basically, I spent the next several years developing my craft and improving my writing skills. By the time I reached my senior year, I was already winning college creative writing contests for both poetry and short stories, and it was around this time that a grand opportunity presented itself to me.

BECOMING FAMOUS

It was 1998 and I had just come across a brochure advertising a poetry competition that was being held in Anaheim, California at the Disney Land Resort. It was called The Famous Poet's Convention. The thing that grabbed my attention was the cash prize being offered. For the grand prize, it was $15,000. The first place winner would walk away with $10,000, second place winner with $5,000, third place winner with $3,000, fourth place winner with $2,000, and fifteen fifth place winners with $1,000 each. This was an international contest, meaning poets were there from all over the world: from Africa, from Europe, from Australia, and from all over the USA. Many of the contestants were college professors, published authors, and professionals (lawyers, doctors, educators, etc.). Ages range from 18 years of age and up (you had to be 18 years of age and up to compete in it). So, basically, I was one of the youngest competitors there. There were around a thousand contestants there. I felt outclassed and out of place, but God showed me favor during that competition.

I remember sitting in the audience listening to the names of the twenty finalists being called one by one. They started with the fifteen fifth place winners. As each name was called, the contestant had to approach the stage, recite their poem, pose with an oversized copy of their check for a picture (the real check was given to them at the end of the awards ceremony), and then take a seat in one of the twenty chairs on the stage. After the fifth place winners' names were called, it was on to the fourth place winner. I just knew it was over for me since I didn't make one of the fifth place slots. I couldn't see myself winning a higher spot. I didn't think my poem was good enough to place higher.

I sat and listened as someone else's name was called for the fourth place spot. I clapped and began collecting the pieces of my shattered ego, preparing to leave the ballroom and go back to my room. The name of the third place winner was called. I clapped. Suddenly, the host got ready to announce the second place winner. *Who could that be?* I thought to myself. A brief silence fell over the room as the announcer got ready to announce the winner:

> "And the second place winner is . . . TIMOTHY FLEMMING, JR.!!"

I was stunned! Floored! Speechless! Beside myself! The moment was surreal. Was I dreaming? The look on my face certainly suggested that I was trapped somewhere between two worlds, floating in limbo. I was being announced as the second place winner and was being handed a jumbo-sized check with my name on it in the amount of $5,000. I read my poem, posed for my picture, then sat down in one of the few remaining chairs on stage, still in shock and disbelief. I had never received such a huge amount of money in my life, but God was still favoring me. I knew God's hand was at play in the situation.

THE BIGGEST CHALLENGE

The following year much of that money had dwindled away thanks to college expenses and a few other expenses. I found myself with only an estimated $1,800 left in my account, and things were about to get a little bit tighter for me. One day, while driving in a mall parking lot, I got into a car accident with another driver. Behind this, I had to go to court to resolve the matter. The judgment I was handed was a $500 fine to pay. On top of this, another semester was getting ready to begin and I was going to need all of my money for books and other things. I had it all figured out in my mind: I would pay this, pay that, give this much, and then attempt to cling onto the rest as if holding on for dear life; and then, that's when God spoke.

Maybe it was due to the fact that I had developed a personal plan regarding the remainder of that money that attracted God; I don't know. Movie director, Woody Allen, is quoted as saying, "If you want to make God laugh, tell him about your plans." I can't argue with his logic. God has been known to laugh at man's plans before in Scripture. He laughed when man said he was going to build a tower whose tip extended into the heavens. God laughed when Pharaoh declared himself to be a god and when King Nebuchadnezzar thought the same thing about himself. God even stated that in Proverbs 1:26 that He will laugh at the calamity that will befall those who ignore His voice. Maybe it was the fact that I had my own plans that caused God to issue this next challenge.

It was a Sunday morning and Pastor Flemming, Sr. was appealing to the congregation to sow a seed offering. I was sitting in the pulpit, contemplating how much to give. My mind was already made up that I was going to sow that morning, but I was cautious regarding the amount, considering that I had court fees, school expenses, and a list of other expenses to take care of with that last little bit of cash in my bank account. The pastor asked for everyone that could to sow a hundred dollars. I was going to impress God, or so I thought. I was going to give two hundred dollars. *I know God is going to be impressed by this*, I thought.

Here is where I pause to remind you that God hates pride and arrogance. When we possess smug attitudes and think that God ought to be impressed by our acts of service and our few dollars, that's when God reminds us that He's not impressed and that we're not as big and bad as we think we are. That's when God gives us the *rich young ruler treatment*...just as He did me. When I pulled out my checkbook to write that check for two hundred dollars, that's when the Holy Spirit came upon me and convicted me and then began speaking to me about another amount He wanted me to give. At that moment, I prayed and asked the Holy Spirit to reveal to me the exact amount He wanted me to sow. Immediately, I received a vision in my head of the total amount that was in my bank account. God was instructing me to sow every penny that was in my bank account—EVERY PENNY! Upon receiving this unction from God, I immediately began rebuking Satan. I just knew God would never instruct a man to empty out his bank account in church because He is a God of order...and common sense. In my soul, I knew that it was God speaking to me to sow that amount of money, but I was hesitant to go along with what He was instructing me to do. After a few seconds of rebuking Satan in my mind, I began to settle down and accept the fact that it wasn't Satan urging me to give; it was God. I dropped my pride and then wrote down the amount God was speaking to me about on a new check. As I got up to give that check I began to think about everything I needed that money for: the court order, my maintenance expenses for my car, money for books, money for gas, etc. Nonetheless, I placed that check in the offering plate as God instructed me to and went back to my seat.

When sowing that seed, I had a strange feeling. On the one hand, I was nervous and afraid, wondering whether or not God was really going to take care of my needs; I was reluctant to part with that money and place myself in such a vulnerable state again; but on the other hand, I felt a sudden peace in my soul. This peace seemed to indicate to me that I had just done not only the right thing, but that I had made the best decision I could have ever made. In my spirit, God reaffirmed to me that my financial sacrifice was in obedience to His will and that I have the right to anticipate a handsome reward. I had a choice at that moment: Do I agree with what I feel in my flesh (fear; doubt) or do I go with what I know in my spirit (that God will honor His promise in my life)? I decided to go along with the latter. I had to remind myself that God is not a liar, that He is more than capable of blessing me and seeing to my needs, that He is not ignorant of all of the expenses I need to take care of, that He is sincerely concerned about my situation, that He sees my faithfulness and obedience, and that I have a humongous blessing coming my way due to my act of obedience to God in the area of giving.

THE BIGGEST MISTAKE WE CAN MAKE AFTER SOWING A FINANCIAL SEED

As I just explained a moment ago, I didn't feel good after I sowed that seed offering of $1,800 plus dollars; actually, the feeling I got was a combination of nausea, fear, regret, and grief...as if I had just lost a loved one. As that check left my hand, I felt like lamenting. As I sat back down in my chair, I had a nearly listless expression on my face as if having gone through some traumatic incident. I couldn't even pay attention to the pastor's sermon that morning because my mind kept replaying that moment over and over again. All I could think about was what I had just parted ways with. I felt as if I had just been stripped naked. I felt a lightness and light-headedness. I knew the Bible said we must give cheerfully because that's what God loves, but I also sensed that God is not out of touch with our feelings in every situation. After all, in the book of Hebrews, we are reminded that Jesus can relate to all of our feelings because He, too, was tempted in all parts as we are although He didn't give in to His temptation and commit sin (4:15). I was reminded that even Jesus sweated thick drops of blood while getting ready to face the cross, something He was already predestined to face. Even Jesus began to pray and ask the Father to allow Him to find another way to secure our salvation rather than suffer in the way He was about to suffer. But, eventually, Jesus switched gears and realigned Himself with the Father's perfect will. He then uttered these words: "...yet, not my will but yours be done" (Luke 22:42). We all feel butterflies in our stomachs when it comes to obeying God, but we can't give in to temptation and obey the flesh over God. Furthermore, it is important that we keep reminding ourselves of God's Word while going through with what He instructs us to do, and also after we've done what He instructed us to do.

Some people will simply sow their seed offerings and then go their way harboring negative feelings and doubts as opposed to challenging these negative thoughts and doubts with the Word of God. Many people forget the importance of maintaining an attitude of faith *after* sowing their seeds.

Hebrews 4:2 says,

> "For unto us was the gospel preached, as well as unto them: but the word preached did not profit them, not being mixed with faith in them that heard it."

Notice here that God provided grace and blessings to many, but the only ones that experienced these blessings were the ones that chose to have an attitude of faith and believe what they heard. What is your attitude when it comes to God's promises? Do you choose to believe what God says or do you choosse instead to doubt what He says? It does no good to act on an instruction from God while doubting Him the whole time. Your acts of service to God must be done in an attitude of faith, which means *to believe God's Word.* It's possible to serve God with the wrong attitude. It's possible to forget that you have to constantly speak God's promises over yourself while waiting for your harvest to come. Paul, the Apostle, told his son in the ministry in 1 Timothy 1:18,

> "Timothy, my son, I am giving you this command in keeping with the prophecies once made about you, so that by recalling them you may fight the battle well..." (NIV)

He told Timothy to constantly remind himself of the prophecies spoken over him in order to fight Satan who wanted to steal the seed of faith from his heart. Remember what Jesus told us about faith in Matthew chapter 13? He explained to us that faith (God's Word and promises) is similar to a seed and it must be protected from the devil. When Satan sees God planting His Word (promises) in someone's heart, Jesus said Satan then "comes and snatches away the seed that was planted in their hearts" due to their lack of understanding and comprehension (13:19, NLT). So, you must protect your faith. Don't let Satan steal your faith. Don't let your heart be filled with doubt because the only way for you to experience the results of financial sowing is to continue believing God, His promises, and His Word. Doubt will cause you to miss God's promises in your life.

Speak over your seed. Remember: You must water a seed if you want it to grow. You can't just place a seed in the ground and then expect it to grow on its own. You have to water it. How do you water a seed in the spirit? You water it by constantly speaking and thanking God for His promises. Get up in every morning and remind yourself of what God has promised you and then begin to thank God for what He promised and what He is about to perform in your life. Praise God before you see the manifestation of what He has promised you. Keep thanking God for your harvest, which is to come. Keep an attitude of faith. And when thoughts of doubt begin to creep up in your mind, cast them down with the Word of God by declaring openly God's promises over your life. All Satan is after is your faith. He knows that if he can steal your faith, he can get you to forfeit what God has for you; he knows that he'll be able to get you to give up the race right before you can cross the finished line and receive your reward.

Hebrews 10:35-36 says,

> "Cast not away therefore your confidence, which hath great recompence of reward. For ye have need of patience, that, after ye have done the will of God, ye might receive the promise."

Patience (or "perseverance" as it is rendered in other translations) is a requirement for receiving from God. Impatience will cause you to get anxious, antsy, and begin to doubt and question God. You have to know that God is true to His Word and that He not only *can* but that He *will* come through for you just as He promised. This assurance is what will enable you to rest comfortably through your season of waiting.

BLESSINGS ARE FOR GROWN-UPS

Trixs may be for kids, but when it comes to the blessings of God, there is a good reason why we experience a season of waiting. James explains it here in this passage of Scripture:

> "My brethren, count it all joy when ye fall into divers temptations; knowing this, that the trying of your faith worketh patience. But let patience have her perfect work, that ye may be perfect and entire, wanting nothing." (James 1:2-4)

In the New Living Translation, this verse is rendered:

> "Dear brothers and sisters, when troubles come your way, consider it an opportunity for great joy. For you know that when your faith is tested, your endurance has a chance to grow. So let it grow, for when your endurance is fully developed, you will be perfect and complete, needing nothing."

Patience—or perseverance, endurance—is the thing that, according to Scripture, establishes character in us. We must learn how to endure and persevere through hardship so that we can develop the right mentality, the kind that enables us to operate in a level of maturity that will allow us to not only gain a blessing but keep that blessing. In essence, most people lose a good thing because they lack the maturity to handle what they've been given; they don't know what they have, and they therefore fail to value what they have. People who work hard to get what they have and get to where they are in life tend to value the opportunities they've been given more than those who don't work as hard for them. One of the surest signs of maturity is gratitude. Immature people pout when they don't get what they want because they think they are entitled to having their way. Mature people, on the other hand, show gratitude for all that they've been given and don't pout because they realize that no one is entitled to a blessing. God blesses people who are grateful, not people who're entitled, spoiled, and love to complain whenever things don't go their way. If you're a complainer, you might want to change your attitude. Complaining and murmuring doesn't draw God's presence and please Him; these things actually repel Him and cause Him to avoid blessing us. Always give thanks for what God has blessed you with, knowing that even life is a blessing according to Acts 17:28, which says, "...For in him (God) we live and move and exist" (NLT). The blessing of life, clean air, oxygen, of hope, of extraordinary possibilities, of love, rest, sleep, food and water, etc. all come from God. On the flip-side of this is the place Jesus talked about extensively in the gospels: hell. We enjoy all of these little blessings on the earth, not realizing that none of them exist in hell, which is the place where the presence of God cannot be found. The Bible says there's no rest in hell, no light in hell (sunlight is a blessing), no food and water in hell, no peace in hell, no love in hell (since God is love according to 1 John 4:8), no hope in hell, no salvation in hell, no sleep in hell, barely any oxygen in hell, no possibilities of a better life or a turnaround in hell, etc. So always be appreciative even of the little things God has given you; and furthermore, learn to show thanks and appreciation for not only the things God has given you but the things you need Him to give you also. As Paul tells us, even when you bring your petitions (specific requests) to God in prayer, do it with "thanksgiving" (Philippians 4:6).

ARE YOU A COMPLAINER OR ARE YOU MATURE?	
Things Complainers Say (The wrong responses)	Things Mature People Say (The right responses)
God, why haven't you blessed me yet?	God, thank you for every blessing you've already given me.
I'm so sick and tired of this.	God, whatever you want to teach me in this situation, do it.
This ain't supposed to happen to me! Not me! Why me?	God, you said to rejoice even in trials and tribulations; therefore, I praise you in the midst of this.
God, where are you?	God, I thank you that you will never leave nor forsake me.
Nothing ever works out for me.	God, I thank you that all things are working together for my good because I love you.
Praise God? For what? What has He done for me lately?	God could've let me die in my sins and go to hell, but He took my punishment on the cross. I'm so grateful for His grace.
I'm so sick and tired of these preachers asking for money. That's all they ever talk about.	If I have it to give, I can; if I don't have it, I can't give it. Oh, well. But I won't deprive those that can of the chance to give.
Why they get to have that blessing? They don't deserve that. That should be mine!	I don't know that person's situation—all they had to go through to get to where they are—but I'm happy for them. I am also excited about what God is about to do in my life.

Chapter Four

Faith Comes by Hearing

One of the misconceptions many people have about giving is that it is a form of bribing or negotiating with God. When we perceive giving in this way, we assume that we bring some bargaining power to the table as if God needs us. God wants us to give to the things of the Kingdom, but He doesn't "need" us. Trust me when I say every instruction God gives us is for our benefit and not His. Salvation is for our benefit, not God's—God's throne is not on the line; God's soul is not in jeopardy. If we don't give for the advancement of the gospel, the only ones who will suffer due to not hearing the gospel are our fellow neighbors. Christ could have allowed all of us to die in our sins, but only because of His love for us He decided to give His life for us on the cross. He didn't have to do it.

We don't have any bargaining power when it comes to God. What can you give Him? Really?! Do you think He needs your money? The pavement where He lives is made out of gold. Do you really think that God needs your voice when He has multitudes of angels to keep Him entertained? These angels sing throughout all eternity with their perfect voices God's praises. God is simply giving you the opportunity to praise Him like His angels do. Please don't tell me you think God needs your expertise or intelligence. Just... don't! Our intelligence is a gift from God.

The things we have to offer God are things God has already given us...including our money. The reason Scripture says it is more blessed to give than it is to receive is because being able to give means you have been blessed with something to give first. You're first a recipient, then a giver.

Which came first: the chicken or the egg? What do you think: the chicken! God made the chicken first and then placed the eggs inside of it so that it can reproduce itself. In the same sense, do you suppose that your seed preceded the blessing? If so, you are wrong. God's blessing came before your seed. How so? If God didn't first give you money, you wouldn't have any to sow. God gave you the talent to develop. God gave you the mind to innovate with. God gave you the breath in your lungs—and the lungs, too. Don't get the wrong idea about giving. If you give, it's only because God blessed and allowed you to give.

Again, the Apostle Paul said God "gives seed to the sower" (2 Corinthians 9:10). God gives seed (money) to the people who have the right plans regarding what to do with it. I can recall several years ago when I was sitting in church and the pastor was asking for the members to approach the altar with their seed offerings. That Sunday morning, all I had was fifty cents in my pocket. At first, I felt embarrassed that that was all I had on me to give. I figured that, as a minister, I should have had much more money to give. *But hey!* So, I overcame my feelings of embarrassment and decided to focus on the biblical principle of seed faith instead. I took that little bit of change out of my pocket, placed it gently in an envelope (trying not to make a lot of noise), and then followed the instruction that was being given over the pulpit, which was to write down on the back of the envelope what I wanted God to do in my life. My prayer request was simple. I wrote on the envelope, "Make me a better sower." That was my prayer. I wanted God to put me in a position where I'd have more money to sow in the seed offering. It's amazing how quickly God moved. That same day, immediately after the service, one of the mothers of the church approached me and handed me a check for fifty dollars. While she was handing me that check, she uttered these words:

> "I don't know why I'm giving this to you, but I just felt led to give this to ya'."

She had no idea that I had just prayed and asked God to give me more money to sow in the seed offering. She was being used by God to provide seed so that I would have more to sow. I then took that check and sowed that money into the ministry that same week.

It is biblical to ask God for seed. Yes, it is! Ask God to give you the finances needed to finance the Kingdom! Do it! Ask Him! Make a promise to God that you will sow from the money He supplies to you. Like Hannah in the Old Testament who made a vow to God that if He gave her a son she would give that son back to Him, we also have the right to go to God and ask Him to bless us with an offering that we can give back to Him. And God will respond. Why? It's because God gives "seed to the sower," not to the hoarder. If God sees that you are willing to use money to serve His will and advance His Kingdom in the earth, then He doesn't see a problem with blessing you with it. Sadly, many people have made promises to God only to fall back on their word. God suddenly blessed you with a job and now you are having second thoughts about giving. God suddenly sent several clients to you and now you are hesitant to tithe out of your profits like you promised. And then, once you lose that job, once the clients stop coming and that stream of income dries up, now you are at the altar begging God to bless you to be in a position to give again. James warned us about this when he wrote,

> "What is causing the quarrels and fights among you? Don't they come from the evil desires at war within you? You want what you don't have, so you scheme and kill to get it. You are jealous of what others have,

> but you can't get it, so you fight and wage war to take it away from them. Yet you don't have what you want because you don't ask God for it. And even when you ask, you don't get it because your motives are all wrong—you want only what will give you pleasure" (James 4:1-3, NLT).

James warned us that you can hustle and grind to try to get ahead and get a blessing, but you won't receive that blessing for one reason: you didn't ask God for it. And yet, after you have asked God for a blessing, due to your motives being in the wrong place, God refuses to bless you. So, ask God for a financial blessing, but make sure your intentions for having it is so that you can serve Him and His will with it as rather than serving yourself.

BID ME TO COME, JESUS!

That particular Sunday morning when the Holy Spirit told me to sow the $1,800 plus that I had in my bank account, it is important to emphasize that the Holy Spirit is who moved on my heart and instructed me to sow that seed. Remember: My decision, my will, my desire was to sow $200. God had something else in mind. That morning, after the conviction of the Holy Spirit fell upon my heart, I had to take the next step and . . . ask God to tell me what to sow. I needed to get clearance from God on what to sow. I couldn't just do what I wanted to do and expect to receive God's best.

The Bible tells us that faith comes through "hearing,

and hearing by the word of God" in Romans 10:17. In that text, the word "word" is rendered *rhēma*, and it means "that which is uttered or spoken by God." It's one thing to read a Bible verse and believe on it and another to hear a direct word of knowledge or word of prophecy from God either in your spirit man or through the mouth of one of God's prophets and believe on that. When God speaks a rhēma word to us, it is a word that directly addresses a situation we are in. The written Word of God (Bible, *logos*) provides an overall context for which we are able to understand God's heart, His mind, His perspective, and His will in the earth, but a spoken word (a rhēma) provides a specific instruction for a specific situation. For example, the written Word provides a basic context for understanding God's overall will, that will being that God doesn't want you to live in debt and poverty, but only through a rhēma word will you receive direct instructions from God on how to get out of debt and overcome poverty. When God speaks to you directly about your specific situation, He might tell you to start a business in another city or state or contact a certain person and mention to them your situation and need(s) or go back to school and get training in a certain field, or He may tell you to sell your house and move to another side of town or quit your job and start a certain business or He might instruct you to turn down a certain job offer despite it offering you more money because He knows that the company is about to hit a certain crisis and go out of business in the upcoming days. That's a direct word (a rhēma). That's what you need. You need a specific word from God, a specific instruction. That's what the Bible means when it says that faith comes by hearing the Word—it's saying faith is established in our hearts when God speaks directly to us and gives us instructions.

Faith comes by hearing both the written Word (logos) and the spoken word (rhēma). The written Word lays the foundation for our faith, the foundational understanding of God's will for our lives; but nowhere in the written Word does God tell you what type of car to buy, which job to take, or what city to live in; but God will send one of His prophets to advise you what you need to do in these unique circumstances, or He will speak directly to your heart as He did mine. One of the distinguishing characteristics of the Christian faith is the fact that we serve a living Savior, one who still interacts with us today; one who sees us, knows us, talks with us and helps us today; one who isn't a relic, statue, or deceased figure. Jesus said we must live by every "word that proceedeth out of the mouth of God" in Matthew 4:4; again, the word "word" is translated *rhēma* in the Greek in that verse. Jesus was saying God never stops talking. God Jehovah, the true and living God, is still speaking today—He speaks to us about His will for us in every situation. The big question is are we listening?

In Matthew 6:8, Jesus told us the Heavenly Father already knows what we need even before we ask Him. God is never caught off guard by our situations; actually, God sees them before they even arrive in our lives. This is why God instructs us to do certain things ahead of time—He is trying to prepare us for storms we don't see yet. He tells us to sow so that we'll have a harvest during the winter seasons of our lives (Proverbs 6:6-8). God sees into our futures; and due to His great love for us, He is always attempting to get us into a blessed place ahead of time. So, it's important to trust that every instruction God gives us is for our own good. God is concerned about our well-being even more than we are. If we truly understood this, we'd never hesitate to follow His guidance, wondering if He's ignoring our immediate needs just to focus on things that don't presently affect us. He sees and He has a plan—He has the ultimate plan. So trust Him.

The mistake that many in society make when rearing our children is we tend to train them into humanism as opposed to a dependency on God. Humanism teaches us to look to ourselves for answers, guidance, and direction, but the Bible urges us to go to God for the answers, guidance, and the direction we need in life. We are not to look within ourselves, but without. We must understand what Solomon wrote: "We can make our own plans, but the LORD gives the right answer" (Proverbs 16:1, NLT). It's not about the plans we make for our own lives; it's about God's plans for our lives. That's what counts. Our prayer should be, "Lord, what do you want me to be? What do you want me to do? What is your calling for my life?" Any plan that God has for your life is guaranteed to come to pass when we rely on His power to bring it into fruition. With God, there are no risks. We have a 100% guarantee of success when pursuing that which God has predestined for us to have. This is where the Law of Faith and the Law of Attraction differs. The Law of Attraction tells us to visualize what we want for our lives and then believe in some mystical power or energy embedded within us to materialize it while faith teaches us to visualize God's plan for our lives and rely on His power to bring it to pass. But the only way to discover God's plan for your life is to seek Him for it.

Only God knows what we're supposed to be and do in this life; after all, we are His handiwork (Ephesians 2:10). When God created us, He placed certain treasures inside of us. But the secret is this: only God knows what is really on the inside of us. We may think we know, but we really don't. Jeremiah explained that our hearts are "deceitfully wicked" and we don't know them; only God knows them (Jeremiah 17:9-10). What God does is search our hearts to reveal to us what is buried within them. Solomon wrote, "The spirit of man is the lamp of the LORD, searching all the innermost parts of his being" (Proverbs 20:27, New American Standard Bible). The Holy Spirit not only digs through our hearts to unveil what hidden treasures lie within us, but He also searches the Father's heart to unveil what hidden plans and intentions for our lives lie in His heart. That's what the Apostle Paul meant when he wrote in 1 Corinthians 2:9-10,

> "That is what the Scriptures mean when they say, 'No eye has seen, no ear has heard, and no mind has imagined what God has prepared for those who love him.' But it was to us that God revealed these things

by his Spirit. For his Spirit searches out everything and shows us God's deep secrets." (NLT)

Developing a relationship with the person of the Holy Spirit is the key to unlocking the revelation of God's will for our lives. As I drew closer to God, He began revealing to me other gifts and talents and passions that He buried inside of me, things I didn't know were there. For example, my focus was originally on the boxing ring, but God knew there was more inside of me, much more. He placed creative writing inside of me among other talents and passions. God not only revealed to me what was inside of me which I didn't know about, but He also spoke to me about His will for my life. My plan was to succeed in the boxing ring; God, however, had a different plan. When I humbled myself one night and prayed for God to reveal His will for my life to me, I immediately received a vision of myself preaching in the pulpit; I instantly knew what my destiny was; I knew where I would be and what I'd be doing in life. This has pretty much been a pattern in my life: Ask God, wait for Him to speak, then move on His instructions. I can only be confident when doing what in my heart I know God has instructed me to do. And I know God didn't call me to the basketball court; He called me to the ministry and to entrepreneurship.

My wife and I will hang around anointed people and stay in settings where God is speaking prophetically. Now, this doesn't justify neglecting to read the Bible for direction. To be honest, if a person is unwilling to pay attention to the written Word of God, then God will not even provide for them a rhēma word for their situation. How do I know this? Because the Bible declares in Hosea chapter four that when we refuse to read God's written Word, He will reject us; and in 2 Timothy 2:15, the Apostle Paul told us that the way we show God that we are serious about being used by Him for His purpose in the earth is that we "study" His Word. The person who rejects the written Word of God is in danger of being rejected by God Himself. So, why should we expect to be instructed by God into a blessing when we won't even follow the instructions He first wrote down for us? When we are in right standing with God according to His written Word, we can anticipate receiving a rhēma Word from God for our specific circumstances. We stay around the fire! That is one of the greatest assets my wife and I have. That is how I discovered not just what area to go in (entrepreneurship), but even what specific type of business to start. That is how I knew I was going to marry at an early age. That is even how I knew who my wife would be, how many children we would have, and what each of those children would be when they reached adulthood. That's how my wife knew what job to take, to quit, and what business to start. That's how we gained the assurance of our futures that allowed us to navigate through the turbulence of our circumstances.

When the twelve disciples were caught in the midst of a storm while on the tumultuous Sea of Galilee in Matthew chapter fourteen, Peter demonstrated faith. While everyone was frightened by the sight of Jesus walking on the water towards their boat, Peter did something unusual: he spoke up and asked,

> "Lord, if it be thou, bid me come unto thee on the water" (vs. 28).

Before Peter made a move, He first asked God to "bid" him, to instruct him, tell him, ask him, command him to come; to step out onto something that he, in his natural, normal state would be incapable of handling. You can do the extraordinary, but only if God graces you to do it. If God tells you to step out on faith to do something, just know that He'll give you the anointing, the strength, the power, and the ability to do it. You can accomplish God's plan for your life because you have God's power enabling you to do so.

That Sunday morning, God led the dance. God told me exactly how much to sow and where to sow. He already planned to bless me, but He needed my obedience to release that blessing in my life. God even gave me the $5000 to sow from. It was all God. I was simply hearing and obeying. It's important that we learn how to do just that: hear and obey. You don't have to come up with a plan and then inform God about what you want and need; He already came up with a plan and knows every step you need to take to accomplish it in your life. Ask Him for a seed. Ask Him for His will daily. Ask Him to guide and instruct you. Let Him bid you to take each step towards your destiny...because ultimately, it's not the water that you'll find yourself walking on, it's the Word.

Chapter Five

It Won't Stop Raining!!!

I sowed a phenomenal seed one Sunday Morning in 1999 and received a huge blessing the next year. I discovered something amazing about God: He doesn't force His will on anyone, but He sure knows how to manipulate the circumstances just to cause us to line up with His will. And it's a good thing when God is in relentless pursuit of you in order to bless you. Imagine God chasing you down just to get money into your hands. I experienced this...over and over again after sowing that one seed of $1,800 plus.

In the year 2000, the Famous Poets Convention sent out another brochure advertising their poetry convention. This time, the stakes were higher. The cash prizes were the same as in the previous year, but this convention was a little bit bigger. There were celebrities who were also poets that were presenting and other celebrities that were performing, we were going to be treated to a nice champaign reception, there would be more workshops, and more. Everything was truly exciting, but for whatever reason I had decided that I wasn't going to attend that convention. In fact, I'd decided that I wasn't going to attend any more conventions, period. Truthfully, I was just afraid that I wouldn't see a repeat of what happened the previous year and would instead end up going home disappointed and empty-handed. I then put that brochure down and forgot about it for a couple of months. The time of the convention was now upon us. My mom approached me about going, but I declined. She then urged me to reconsider sitting this one out, so I prayed about it, and after praying about the matter, my heart felt inclined to go. But there was a problem: the plane tickets were too expensive—they were over $1,000 per ticket roundtrip. There was another problem: the hotel where the convention was being held (in Reno, Nevada) was completely booked up. There were no more rooms available, especially at the discounted rate provided to the convention attendees. All of this bad news began to discourage me and reinforced in my mind my earlier position that I should just stay home and don't take the risk. But God had other plans.

It was the week before the convention was scheduled to start and I didn't have a plane ticket nor a room, but all of a sudden, the circumstances began to change. All of a sudden, at the last minute, the plane tickets dropped in price from over one thousand dollars to around $280 roundtrip. I certainly didn't want to pass up that opportunity, so took a step of faith and purchased the tickets, not really knowing what to do about the situation with the hotel. But God had that covered also. At the very last minute, one of the guests who was participating in the convention pulled out, leaving one room at the discounted rate available. Well, that problem was now solved. I had plane tickets and a room all at a low cost. So, off to Reno my mom and I went.

My mom and I arrived in Reno, Nevada. It was in the month of October and it was cold. Real cold. The frigid air and rushing winds made for a deadly combination, especially considering that I didn't dress adequately for them. I had a light jacket, thinking that Nevada would be hot. We then arrived at our hotel—this was the Hilton Hotel. It was huge. Fabulous. Of course, this was the first hotel I had seen that had its own shopping mall, theater, bowling alley, mini theme park, night clubs, and full casino inside of it. *It would have been perfect had it not been for all of the cigarette smoke. But hey, it's Reno!* My mom and I checked in then settled in. The room was beautiful. We then headed to the convention area to check in and grab our registration packets. When we went downstairs to the registration area, it was so gorgeous...and huge. Furthermore, the place was packed. This convention was nearly double the size of the previous year's convention. We encountered a sea of people at the registration station and beyond. After a few hours of waiting in line to get our registration packets, we proceeded to the ballroom where the champagne reception was being held. This was one of the largest and most beautiful ballrooms I had ever seen in my life. It spoke of luxury, of class, of money. The decor was spectacular. The set up was splendorous. It amazed me how so much money flowed through that place. Thousands of people filled that ballroom. There were way more poets to compete against this year. The reception got on its way. Everything was upbeat, fun, and exciting. The presentation was top-notch. After the reception, all of the poets were instructed to go to their assigned rooms where they would interact with their instructors during the convention over the next three days. Each "home-room" had around a hundred or more poets in it. We all had a schedule laying out the workshops times and events. Workshops went on throughout the majority of the day and they were a lot of fun. But the judging process was what was different this year. This year, the poets had to select among each other in their own home-rooms the three poets they thought should enter the winner's circle. Everyone had been provided with ballot sheets and given the opportunity to recite our poems in front of our home-rooms and instructors; and afterward, the instructors had to retrieve each ballot sheet (along with their own) and submit them to the final judges. The judging panel was made up of about eight people. They were mainly published authors, professional poets, and the likes.

On the second day of the convention, each group of poets had to present in front of the final panel of judges. Of course, this was the nerve-wracking part. I was so nervous I couldn't stop shaking. The scene was more intimate than in the previous convention. We didn't have to get up and recite our poems in front of the entire convention; instead, it was just the judges and us and the handful of people who decided to sit in on our presentations. When my name was called, I stepped onto the stage and then recited my poem. We were only allowed one minute to recite our poems and each poem had to be twenty-one lines or less. I can appreciate this rule in light of the fact that there were around two thousand poets competing in that convention; so imagine if everyone decided to read two page-long poems which took five to ten minutes each to recite. We would still be dealing with the preliminaries to this day.

I read my poem and then exited the stage, not knowing what was going to happen, not knowing what to think. I just hoped they liked the poem. I hoped my home-room and instructor like my poem. If I'd gone home empty-handed, I was prepared to deal with it. It was still a fun ride.

After the judging phase was over, everyone was getting ready for the big banquet. Everyone got dressed up and headed to the big ballroom which, again, was gorgeously decorated. The food was exquisite. Everything was wonderful. That evening's entertainment was Phyllis Diller, a famous comedian and actress. I'd never heard of her before then, but she had everyone laughing. She was quite funny. After the banquet, everyone turned in for the night to get some rest. The next day was the big day—it was the awards ceremony where the winners were going to be announced.

The next day came. I got up out of bed and prepared

myself for the awards banquet. In my mind, I figured that I was going to return home with nothing but memories of the convention to store in the chamber of my heart, but not any money—at least, not any big money. Again, my hope was to at least land in one of the fifteen fifth place slots, which yielded a $1,000 prize. The ceremony went this way: First, twenty door prizes were given out to those with winning raffle ticket. Door prize winners graced the stage to receive their prizes, which consisted of either a free book publishing deal or a free registration for two for the following year's convention. After the door prizes were given it was time for that which we all came for: the announcement of the twenty money winning poets. This time, the facilitators did things a little differently than in the previous year. This time, rather than announcing the placement of the winners first, the host simply called all twenty winners to the stage first, had them sit down in the twenty chairs on the stage (no particular order), and then he began announcing their placements one by one, starting with all the fifth place winners. One by one their names were called and they approached the podium, read their poems, received the oversized show-checks, posed for the camera, and went back their seats on the stage.

My name was called among the twenty winners. I then graced the stage and took a seat. As the fifth place winners were being called, I was shocked that my name wasn't called among them. I figured that maybe I would receive the fourth place winning and take home $2,000, but then someone else's name was called. Well, that left four more slots to fill. When it was time for the third place winner's name to be called, my heart began to race because I just knew my name was going to be called and I was going to be going home with a check in the amount of $3,000. Drumroll!!!!! "And the third place winner is . . ." It wasn't me! *Wow!* I thought. *I'm actually going to win second place again and go home with $5,000*, I thought. At this time, there were only three slots left and only three of us left on the stage whose names had not been called. My heart wasn't beating very fast because I knew my name was getting ready to be called as the second place winner. I then scooted to the edge of my chair, ready to get up as my name was being announced for second place. Drumroll!!! "And the second place winner is . . . ." *What?!!! It's not me?!!!* I thought to myself. Someone else's name was called as the second place winner. I nearly sunk into my chair. My mind was swirling. I couldn't even think. All I knew was there were only two spots left and two people left on stage whose names had not been called: mine and another lady's. Also, there were only two slots left: first place and the grand prize. All I knew was there were only two cash prizes left to be handed out: a first place winning of $10,000 and a grand prize winning of $15,000. At this point, I felt like I was floating in limbo. I could see my mom in the audience. She was just as much in a state of shock and disbelief and I was. The only thing that snapped me back to reality was the sound of the drumroll which, at that point, I didn't even care about. I was about to go home from that convention with $10,000 or more—*and I wasn't even going* *to attend that convention out of fear*. God had to make me go by performing little miracles to get me there.

Drumroll!!!!! "And the first place winner, the winner of our $10,000 prize is . . . TIMOTHY FLEMMING, JR.!!!" I walked—or more like floated—to the podium, recited my poem, grabbed my show-check, posed for my picture, went back to my seat and just basked in the moment. I could only think of one thing: "God is paying me back for the seed that I sowed last year."

I wish I could say that this is where the story ends, but I can't. The story doesn't end there. God wasn't through.

THE DOOR PRIZE

I returned to the Famous Poets Convention in 2002, but this time I didn't make the big money slots; instead, I came in fifth place, winning $1,000. The next year, I got married to my beautiful wife. In 2004, me and my wife, Jackie, attended that year's convention. During that convention something interesting happened: I was approached by one of the facilitators at the convention and asked to attend a special session in the main ballroom. When I arrived at the ballroom, I was ushered to the main stage where around nine other poets were seated. We were presented to the entire convention as the top winners of the Famous Poets Convention. The host then singled me out and read my 1998 second place winning poem before the audience. After the presentation, each of us on stage was left to interact with the conference attendees and sign autographs—every registrant had been given an anthology featuring the convention's past winners. The audience members flooded the stage to get our autographs. After a while of autographing books, my arm started to get tired. When I looked up, I noticed that I had a line wrapped around the ballroom waiting for my autograph. I really felt famous at the moment. At the time, two beautiful young ladies approached me for my autograph. While autographing their books, one of them asked me, "Do you mind if I ask you a question?"

"Sure," I responded.

"What is your number one goal, your ultimate purpose in life?"

I looked at the young lady and replied, "To do the will of God for my life." Just that answer alone resonated in her spirit. The young lady was amazed by my answer. It truly blessed her. I began to think to myself, *This is why God exalts us to positions of influence. This is what we're supposed to do whenever God places us in a position where we have a spotlight: glorify God and point others to Christ.*

Now, it was the last day of the conference and it was time for the awards ceremony. Let me stop and warn you to be careful about uttering words and stating your plans. Like I said before, God tends to take it as a personal challenge to remind us of who is really in control. Before the host began to announce the twenty door prizes, I remember leaning over to my wife and saying, "This is my last time attending this conference. I'm not returning anymore." I felt as if the ride, although fun, was time to come to an end, at least for me. I figured I'd won enough and been blessed enough, or so I thought.

The twenty door prizes were now being announced. The system was the same: every attendee had been given a raffle ticket and the corresponding raffle tickets had been kept and placed into a spinning drum tumbler, which a facilitator began to spin with all of the tickets therein. The facilitator then called for a volunteer out of the audience to reach into the tumbler and read off the ticket numbers. Now, I had just declared that I wasn't going to return to the convention anymore, but I can imagine God saying, *Oh, really? We'll see about that.* As the ticket numbers were being read, guest whose ticket number got called. That's right. Mine. Out of nearly two thousand attendees, what are the odds that they just happened to pull my ticket out of the wheel? And guess what was my prize. I won a free registration for me and a guest to return to the next year's convention. All I could do was eat my words—I had put my foot in my mouth as the saying goes. I pretty much had no other choice but to return to the convention the following year.

I placed fifth again. I left that year's convention with a $1,000 and a voucher for a free registration for the following year's convention, which was also $1,000 in value. I was now fully convinced that God was up to something.

HERE WE GO AGAIN

I returned to the convention the next year—it was the 2005 Famous Poets Convention. My wife and I arrived there in

Reno, Nevada, ready to go through the motions. This time, I was little late getting my poem in to the judges. I changed my submission poem at the last minute. At the last minute, I received the inspiration to write a totally different poem; I was literally writing it on the plane while flying out to the convention. The title of the poem was *Magdalene Suit.*

The rules of the contest were the same. Everything was pretty much the same. There were only two differences in that year's convention: during the awards ceremony, rather than calling out the names of the twenty winners first and then announcing their placements, the host called each winner and their placement at the same time; also, the cash prizes were different. This year, the first place winning was only $5,000, but the grand prize was now $25,000. The host began calling the seventeen third place winners (of $1,000 each). As each name was called, the winners had to recite their poems, pose with their show-checks for a picture, and then take a seat on the stage in the order they were called. All of the third place winners' names had been announced; and now, it was time for the second place winner's name to be called. Everyone in the audience was held in suspense over who it would be, over who'd be called out of the audience next. The winner's name was finally called. Again, it wasn't mine name called. My heart wasn't racing as intensely as it had in previous conventions. I didn't expect to win anything. I simply expected this round to be a fun ride. But I was open to winning something. Now, it was time for the first place winner to be called from the audience. Everyone held their breaths. When the person's name was called, everyone sighed. Now, it was time for the big prize, the grand prize. Drumroll!!!! The host then said,

> "And now, for our grand prize winner. The grand prize winner for this year's Famous Poets Convention is . . . MAGDALENE SUIT! No, hold up. I'm sorry. That's the name of the poem. The poet's name is...TIMOTHY FLEMMING, JR.!!!"

For a moment, I just dropped my head. This time, it wasn't shocking. This time, I didn't feel like I was trapped in limbo or stuck in a surreal moment. This time, I was well aware of where I was and why I was there. This time, I knew beyond a shadow of a doubt that this was a divine set-up. There was a warmness and an assurance that rested over my soul. I wasn't shocked by the divine providence of God; instead, I was humbled by it. All I could do was praise God and think about His faithfulness to His promise.

When I approached the podium, the first words that fell from my lips were "Glory to God." When I said that, the place erupted in applause. Some people were cheering. I just stood there for a few seconds, humbled by the revelation that when God has you on His mind, when He wants to bless you, when He is determined to bless you, there's no barrier that can stop Him, no hoop He can't and won't jump through, no mountain nor challenge He will not overcome, no ocean He will not cross; He'll change the numbers in the computer and cause the plane tickets to drop suddenly; He will place you on the minds of people, people who can usher you into a season of unparalleled blessings; He will position your raffle ticket directly in the path of a person's hand and cause them to pick it up even in the midst of thousands of other tickets; He will speak to random strangers' hearts and cause them to hunt you down just to place money into your hands; He'll even make your enemies bless you. When God wants to bless you, there's nothing that can stop Him. And when God begins to bless you, the only way I can describe it is this way: *God does exceedingly beyond what we can ask or even imagine.*

There's a season set aside for you as a result of your obedience to God in the area of giving. The only thing that I can advise you to do is bring an umbrella—it's not going to be a light drizzle.

Chapter Six

Cultivating The Soil

I've experienced blessings of all kinds as a result of seeds sown in faith. Some seeds have yielded a harvest quicker than others. Some have taken a little longer than others. Some I'm still anticipating. Occasionally, God will reaffirm to me in my spirit that something phenomenal is on its way. From time to time, God will speak that word to me through one of His prophets, through a lowly saint in a building or on the street in passing. God won't allow me to forget what's coming. He's cooking something big! Real big! I'm excited about it! What a way to live your life. What a blessing it is to always be overcome with incredible excitement, knowing that any day something mindblowingly awesome is about to drop into your lap. And by now, I have come to understand God. I know that sounds strange, but I have. What I've come to expect from God is that He always does things in an unconventional way, that He always does the unexpected. Not knowing where to look only adds to the excitement and the suspense; it keeps your heart pumping and your mind swirling. God loves to keep us in such suspense. He loves to see the expressions on our faces when we stumble into unexpected blessings. We knew they were coming, we just didn't know how they were coming.

According to the Bible, it is God's pleasure to bless us. In fact, the Apostle Paul said it this way:

> "Now all glory to God, who is able, through his mighty power at work within us, to accomplish infinitely more than we might ask or think." (Ephesians 3:20, NLT)

God always does more than we ask Him to. He always looks for ways to blow our minds. It's in His nature. He can't help it. It's important that we know that it is God's will to bless us and prosper us; but more importantly, He doesn't want us to lose sight of Him and His Kingdom agenda and turn His blessings into idols. The blessings of God in our lives are for the purpose of enhancing our lives and witnessing to unbelievers.

When our hearts are in the right place and our motives are in alignment with God's heart, there is nothing He won't give us when we ask. The amazing thing is when we allow God to transform our hearts, our hearts will automatically desire God's will for our lives; and when we therefore pray and bring our petitions before the Lord, we'll already be praying for that which God already intends to give us as explained in Philippians 2:13 and Psalm 37:4. This is why in 1 John 5:14-15, John tells us that we already have that which we ask God for the moment we ask. There's no question of whether or not God is going to say yes. It's a guarantee. We are asking Him for what He wants us to ask Him for.

God cultivates the soil of our hearts before He leads us to sow our seeds. He corrects our motives. He transforms our thinking according to His Word (Romans 12) so that we are focused on His will. He removes all of the elements that hinder our seed from growing and flourishing as revealed in Matthew chapter 13.

THE SOIL OF OUR HEARTS

Another big misconception people have when it comes to sowing seed offerings is they believe the effectiveness of the seed is determined only by the purity of the ministry or the individual they're sowing into, but that's not the case. Yes, it is important to sow into the right place, but here's the big secret many don't know: It's actually the condition of your heart that determines whether or not your seed produces or doesn't produce. It's not merely where you so, but from where you sow that matters. Sowing from an heart that's in the wrong condition will render no results. Let's examine what the Bible says about the condition of our hearts.

In Matthew chapter thirteen, Jesus talks about our

hearts. He said,

> "He told many stories in the form of parables, such as this one: 'Listen! A farmer went out to plant some seeds. As he scattered them across his field, some seeds fell on a footpath, and the birds came and ate them. Other seeds fell on shallow soil with underlying rock. The seeds sprouted quickly because the soil was shallow. But the plants soon wilted under the hot sun, and since they didn't have deep roots, they died. Other seeds fell among thorns that grew up and choked out the tender plants. Still other seeds fell on fertile soil, and they produced a crop that was thirty, sixty, and even a hundred times as much as had been planted!'" (Matthew 13:3-8, NLT)

There are four heart-conditions Jesus emphasized here: a heart that's disinterested in the Word of God, a shallow or stony heart that won't allow God's Word to take root in it, a thorny heart that's filled with too many other cares to let the Word of God flourish, and a heart that is fertile enough for the Word of God to grow in. Let's look at these conditions in more detail:

1. *A disinterested heart.* This heart hears the World of God but doesn't take interest in it. This person lets the Word of God go in one ear and out of the other; their mind isn't concerned about God's truth. Perhaps, this person is interested

only in what they want—in that which their flesh desires—and if one were to talk to them about God, they would just shew them off. They don't see the value of having God in their lives. They don't see the value in reading and living according to God's Word. This describes the person who only wants to receive a blessing from God but has no interest in drawing close to God in their own life. They actually think they can just give a couple of dollars in church and expect God to bless their socks off while they continue to live in deliberate sin and disobedience to His Word. They're terribly mistaken.

The Bible says in Proverbs 15:8,

> "The LORD detests the sacrifice of the wicked, but he delights in the prayers of the upright." (NLT)

Also, in John 9:31, we find these words:

> "We know that God doesn't listen to sinners, but he is ready to hear those who worship him and do his will." (NLT)

So, God doesn't want to hear any other prayer from a sinner besides the prayer of repentance. David told us that when he said in Psalm 51:17 that the one sacrifice God will never reject from us is a "broken and contrite (repentant) heart".

You must first seek to live to please God before asking for His blessings.

2. *A shallow or stony heart*. This heart is unwilling to allow God's Word to completely penetrate it. This is the individual who chooses to believe some of God's Word, but not all of it. They choose to resist the parts of the Word of God that challenge them in certain areas in their lives. For example, this is the person who willingly agrees with God when He speaks against stealing, but they refuse to agree with the passages of Scripture that condemn fornication (sexual immorality). They refuse to let God's Word completely penetrate their heart. They want to argue with the Word when it comes to the areas of their lives they don't want to change. They fight and argue with the Word when it comes to the things they don't want to let go of.

James 1:21 says,

> "So get rid of all the filth and evil in your lives, *and humbly accept the word God has planted in your hearts*, for it has the power to save your souls." (NLT)

How do you react when the Word of God challenges you in a certain area? Do you humble yourself and receive it or do you argue and resist it? Do you try to reason and rationalize sin and come up with excuses for remaining in it rather than letting it go? If you're resistant to the Word of God in your life then your pride will taint and corrupt your seed, making it ineffective when sown. Partial obedience is disobedience.

3. *A thorny heart.* Some people started out serving God with sincere hearts but then they allowed their hearts to be distracted by too many other things, thereby losing their focus. Thorns here are essentially distractions that steal our attention and focus away from God.

Not only are thorns representative of distractions in this passage of Scripture, but they're also representative of ideological contaminants such as false doctrines or heresies, ungodly traditions, and occultic practices. These things will contaminate the soil of our souls and choke the life out of the Word of God in our lives.

The Apostle Paul warns us not to try to mix faith with strange beliefs from mythology. He wrote, "As I urged you when I went into Macedonia, stay there in Ephesus so that you may command certain people not to teach false doctrines any longer or to devote themselves to myths and endless genealogies. Such things promote controversial speculations rather than advancing God's work—which is by faith" (1 Timothy 1:3-4, NIV). This most notably describes many of the ideas put forth in today's secret societies and cults. But the main emphasis is one authenticity of the Christian faith. Paul was explaining that any doctrine that is not of the Bible is a false doctrine that will mislead us and cause our faith to become "shipwrecked" (vs. 19). We can't mix our Christian faith with other faiths. We can't combine elements of Christianity with Hinduism, Buddhism, Islam, Wicca, and other cults and beliefs. Let your faith remain pure.

Paul even wrote in Galatians 1:6-8, “I am astonished that you are so quickly deserting the one who called you to live in the grace of Christ and are turning to a different gospel—which is really no gospel at all. Evidently some people are throwing you into confusion and are trying to pervert the gospel of Christ. But even if we or an angel from heaven should preach a gospel other than the one we preached to you, let them be under God’s curse!” (NIV). Even if an angel were to try to present to you some other doctrine other than that which is recorded in the Bible, Paul says that angel will be cursed by God. Let no one add to, take away, or try to change the wording in God’s Word to support some other belief system.

God warns us not to engage in occultic practices in Deuteronomy 18:10-11, which reads: “Let no one be found among you who sacrifices their son or daughter in the fire, who practices divination or sorcery, interprets omens, engages in witchcraft, or casts spells, or who is a medium or spiritist or who consults the dead” (NIV). So, mixing these practices with your faith as a Christian is strictly forbidden. This is what God indicted the Christians in Acts 19:18-19. In that passage, Luke records that after a mighty display of demonic activity in that town (of Corinth), the Christians realized they needed to repent and get back to God lest demons continued to operate with authority over them. Luke wrote, “Many of those who believed now came and openly confessed what they had done. A number who had practiced sorcery brought their scrolls together and burned them publicly. When they calculated the value of the scrolls, the total came to fifty thousand drachmas" (NIV). The Christians in that town were trying to mix their faith with occult practices, and as a result of this they were powerless against demons. To repent, they brought all of their books of spells and incantations and other occult books and materials and burned them. The dollar value of all of these books combined ranged into the millions of dollars. After they repented of their witchcraft and occultism, the Bible says, "So the word of the Lord grew mightily and prevailed" (New King James Version). This means the Word of God was ineffective in the lives of these Believers because they were mixing it with occult practices.

Jesus said to the Pharisees in Mark 7:13, "Making the word of God of none effect through your tradition, which ye have delivered: and many such like things do ye." In this passage, Jesus explains that ungodly traditions can cause the Word of God to become ineffective in our lives. Just like the other items mentioned in this section, manmade traditions oftentimes choke the life out of God's Word. Some people are more dedicated and committed to their denominations and even their favorite personalities than they are to the Bible, and this has an astounding effect on their seed, a negative one. If your faith is being choked by occultic practices, false doctrines, manmade traditions and ideologies then the seed you sow will be negatively affected by these things.

4. *Fertile hearts.* This is the heart that is soft enough for the

Word to fully penetrate it, deep enough for God's Word to grow roots in it, and clean enough for God's Word to avoid contamination. Whenever a person with this type of heart sows a financial seed into the Kingdom of God, their seed produces results. This person's prayers produce results.

Now, in this Believer, the Word produces the same results but with varying degrees: thirty, sixty, and one hundred fold. What does this mean? It means the Word of God will produce according to the degree of the Believer's level of maturity and understanding in the Word. Jesus explained in verse fifteen that the key to the seed in the fertile heart is the degree of understanding (comprehension) that one has of the Word. For some Believers, their level of maturity (understanding of God's Word) is still in the infancy stage. Their hearts are pure but they're still lacking in knowledge. They don't fully know what they're doing and why. So, we can sow a seed, but if we are not fully mature in our understanding of the Word, then our seed won't yield a stronger yield (a sixty or hundred fold).

The writer of Hebrews explained,

> "You have been believers so long now that you ought to be teaching others. Instead, you need someone to teach you again the basic things about God's word. You are like babies who need milk and cannot eat solid food. For someone who lives on milk is still an infant and doesn't know how to do what is right. Solid food is for those who are mature, who through

> training have the skill to recognize the difference between right and wrong." (NLT)

Remember what Paul wrote in Galatians chapter four about being under teachers and tutors until you reach the level of maturity where you're finally able to handle the inheritance you've been promised. To put it all together, this is what we must consider: Our level of maturity in the Word determines our level of fruitfulness in the faith; and when we are more mature, we become more authoritative and powerful, and are even given more responsibility by God. God is able to trust us with more when we have a greater level of understanding in His Word.

When a person is content with remaining an infant in the faith, refusing to grow in understanding of the Word, they only do themselves a disservice. They cause their own inheritance to remain held up and in the hands of others (or as Paul called them: guardians, tutors, teachers) until we get to that level of maturity to handle those blessings. Some of us complain that God doesn't hear us and doesn't want to bless us, but that's not the case. In reality, God can't bless many of us because we refuse to grow up as Believers. God is only doing what a father does: making sure we're mature enough to drive before handing us the keys to the car. Who would dare place car keys in the hands of a child, especially one still on the bottle, and tell them to take the car for a test drive? When you choose to get off the bottle that is when you'll see greater results.

Your seed is effected by the measure of faith behind it, but each measure is different. The Bible says,

> "For through the grace given to me I say to everyone among you not to think more highly of himself than he ought to think; but to think so as to have sound judgment, as God has allotted to each a measure of faith." (NASB)

There are different measures of faith. In verse 6 of this same passage Paul spoke of the "proportion of faith" given to us by God to operate in various gifts and callings. Faith is a gift from God according to 1 Corinthians 12:9. There's a difference between the faith to believe unto salvation and what Paul referred to as the "gift of faith" in this passage. The gift of faith is the supernatural ability to believe for something spectacular. God will place this kind of faith in your heart so that you can believe Him specifically for something big. God has to anoint you to operate in a particular office in the ministry (the five-fold offices spoken of in Ephesians the fourth chapter). Likewise, God has to give you the measure of faith needed for a certain situation. Faith is produced by the amount of divine revelation one receives from the Word and not by one's intellect. God has to give you revelation; you can't gather it or come up with it on your own. Greater revelation leads to a greater measure of faith; a greater measure of faith leads to a greater yield of fruit; the more fruitful we are in our faith and understanding of God's Word, the more effective our seed becomes. You must first become fruitful in your understanding in order to become fruitful in your sowing and reaping. Solomon warned of the dangers of giving in ignorance. He wrote in Ecclesiastes 5:1,

> "Guard your steps when you go to the house of God. Go near to listen rather than to offer the sacrifice of fools, who do not know that they do wrong." (NIV)

The New Living Translation words it this way:

> "As you enter the house of God, keep your ears open and your mouth shut. It is evil to make mindless offerings to God."

As you continue to draw closer to God, He'll give you more and more understanding and revelation of His Word; and as you grow in understanding and revelation of God's Word, your seed will produce greater results faster. Just know that some of the things that you're believing God for as a Believer whose heart is fertile God is developing and maturing you for. Grow. Enjoy the process. Learn what you must in this season. You're being prepared for the blessing.

WHERE TO SOW

Now that we've established the importance of the condition of your heart, now we'll look at the importance of sowing in the right place.

Before you sow a seed, the first thing you must do is pray and ask the Holy Spirit where to sow. This is extremely important. The Holy Spirit knows when and where you need to sow in order to gain results. Secondly, when sowing financial seed, it is important that you sow according to the principles of the Bible. Here are a few principles that should guide your sowing:

- *The prophet's reward principle*: I'll sow into a vessel of God who blesses my life and is operating in the power of God based off of the Matthew 10:41 principle that declares, "Whoever welcomes a prophet as a prophet will receive a prophet's reward, and whoever welcomes a righteous person as a righteous person will receive a righteous person's reward" (NIV). I understand as Saul in the Old Testament understood that you should always be prepared to sow into an anointed man or woman of God when they minister to you (1 Samuel 9:6-7).

- *The divine revelation principle*: I'll sow into a ministry or teacher of the Word who enlightens my understanding of the Word of God through the sharing of divine revelation. This is based off of Galatians 6:6, which tells us to share in all good things with those who feed us the Word of God. I'm sowing into the Word ministered as a way of both agreeing with it and activing it in my life, understanding that I must choose to believe and act upon that which I heard through an act of faith.

- *The Jewish blessing principle*: I'll sow into ministries and Christian organizations that are involved in evangelizing and providing outreach to the Jewish people, which God calls the "apple of His eye" in Zechariah 2:8. This is based off of Psalm 122:6, which tells us those who pray for the Jewish people and the peace of Israel shall prosper. There's no greater service that one can render to the Jewish people than to lead them to the Messiah, Jesus the Christ, while seeing about their physical needs.

- *The poor and needy principle*: I'll sow into ministries and organizations that are taking care of the poor and needy based off of the principle in Proverbs 19:17, which tells us whoever lends to the poor lends to God and God will repay them. I especially focus on Christian-based organizations that are involved in humanitarian aid.

- *The family first principle*: I'll especially sow into the organizations and ministries involved in providing aid to the suffering, needy, and persecuted Christians at home and abroad, acknowledging the 2 Corinthians 9:12-14 principle and the Galatians 6:10 principle, both of which express that we should take care of family before we try to take care of everyone else—in this case, family being our fellow Believers, members of the body of Christ.

- *The influential people principle*: I'll sow into the lives and ministries or organizations of those I desire to connect with, learn from, receive an impartation from, and even sit under according to the verse in Proverbs 18:16 which tells us our gifts will make room for us and bring us before great and mighty people ("gift" in this passage refers to an offering given to someone else, not a talent or ability that one possesses).

There are a few conditions that I have also observed that are usually present whenever I've sown in the past. For example, as we well know, a seed can't germinate if the conditions aren't conducive to growth. So, these environments have always provided for me a greater sense of comfort as it pertains to sowing: God's anointing is in the atmosphere, the Word of God is being ministered effectively, the foundational doctrine of that which I'm sowing into is sound (built solely on God's Word), Christ is in the center, divine revelation is flowing and bringing about a transformation in my thinking, and there is a freedom that only comes from the presence of the Holy Spirit reigning in the environment. But remember: the main key in effective sowing is to follow the Holy Spirit's guidance. He will never lead you to sow in an environment, a place, or a person that operates outside of His will. The Holy Spirit is the key to it all. He's the one who makes the difference (1 Corinthians 3:7).

Chapter Seven

Blessings To Expect As A Sower

A SEED PRODUCES A HARVEST, BUT WHAT EXACTLY does that mean? Really? When some people today think of a harvest, they picture a single crop. But a harvest is an accumulation of crops in a single season. For our purposes, a harvest is an accumulation of blessings in a single season of one's life. This means two things: a harvest is characterized by the immensity of its quantity and it has a season assigned to it.

There is a season assigned to us when we sow. Paul, the Apostle talked about a season of blessings in Galatians chapter six, and the Apostle Peter talked about it in 1 Peter chapter five. Both Paul and Peter, however, mentioned that there is a process each of us must go through before we enter into that extraordinary season. The blessing is when we sow into God's Kingdom, He will begin to take us through the steps necessary to walk into this incredible season.

PREPARING FOR YOUR SEASON

In Matthew chapter 25, Jesus elaborated on the principle of sowing and reaping when He talked about the three men who had been given a portion of money by their master to invest. One servant was given ten talents, another was given five talents, and the last was given one talent. Now, a talent here refers to a large sum of money. One talent was equivalent to six thousand drachmas or denarii, which were Roman and Greek silver coins. The dollar equivalent of one talent today would be at around $4,000. So, in essence, the master of the house gave to one man an estimate of $40,000, another man an estimate of $20,000, and the last man an estimate of $4,000, and he told each man to invest his money so that when he returned he would see a return on his investments. This is the biggest point most people miss in this story: Jesus said the master gave to each man "according to his ability." The master didn't dare dump money into the hands of someone who wasn't skilled enough to handle it. In this same way, God doesn't just dump a harvest on us; He prepares us for it first by placing us on a path of discovery. When you sow into God's house, prepare for God to cultivate a desire for His will in your heart. The Bible declares,

> "For God is working in you, giving you the desire and the power to do what pleases him."—Philippi-

ans 2:13, NLT

God is going to turn your heart in a new direction, causing you to develop a desire to operate in the area where He has ordained that you succeed in. As you spend more time with God, your heart will continue to desire the very things that He predestined for you to have (Psalms 34:4). Perhaps, one of the worse things in life is to have misplaced desires and to waist your time pursuing after that which is not predestined for you. God has to redirect your desires, your heart.

Another thing God is going to do in your life after you sow into His Kingdom is give you understanding in the area of your place of blessings. Understanding is where the Holy Spirit puts you on a quest for knowledge and information that will enable you to successfully handle what God is about to bestow upon you. Again, God will guide you to the information you need and the mentors you need to receive His blessings. Realize that not all knowledge is good for you and not every mentor is assigned to you. This must be God ordained and inspired in your life. God will mature you.

When it was prophesied to me that I was to go in the area of entrepreneuralship and enter the cash flow market, I had no idea at first what that meant, but then I set out to get knowledge of what that meant. I find it interesting that God didn't just download into my head the knowledge. I find it interesting that God didn't give me all of the details either of what I was supposed to be doing. He gave me a piece of the revelation and then set my feet upon a path to pursue the rest of the information. God placed me on a quest and led me to seminars and trainings, purchasing programs and books, sitting under success coaches, investing thousands of dollars just to gather the information needed. The journey requires a sacrifice of your time and money. Anything that's handed to you, you tend not to appreciate; so God makes us work a little bit in order to get to where we need to be. He, of course, does the hard work on our behalves—He sets the circumstances and puts the people and resources in place for us—but we have to make the small sacrifices and be willing to show up. It is entirely up to us whether or not we watch television or we get up off of the couch and go to where the Holy Spirit is leading us.

During my journey—which, by the way, is a process in itself—God began to teach me about investments. Along the journey, I learned about the importance of developing a vision for my life, about goal-setting, investment opportunities, about the different types of businesses to start, about-growing a business, about different financial accounts, and more. And the most amazing part is when I began studying the principles of success presented by today's gurus of success, I found it fascinating that all of them, both Christian and non-Christian alike, all use the Bible as their model for success. None of them quote from the Qur'an or from any other source. Many of them would take the principles from the Bible and then repackage them as some sort of "secret" and then sell them. But the principle of the imagination, of creating and writing out a vision, of "attracting" wealth by first posturing and perceiving yourself as a person of wealth and influence (or as the Bible says: "As a man thinketh, so is he"—Proverbs 23:7), of establishing your name and reputation before seeking after money, of becoming an "expert" (a person who's very knowledgable in a certain field) rather than a person who's hungry for money, of avoiding and getting out of debt, of investing financially, of seeking mentorship and counsel before making decisions, and of looking to the unseen realm for supernatural help and guidance didn't originate with Napoleon Hill, Earl Nightingale, Vincent Norman Peale, Toney Robbins, John Maxwell, Zig Ziglar, Jim Rohn, or any other success coach or guru on the planet today; these principles originated in the Bible.

THE SCHOOL OF GREATNESS

In Galatians chapter four, the Apostle Paul said that every promise of God is off limits to those who are still child-like in their thinking and void of understanding of God's principles and precepts. As I stated before in another chapter, God places us in a season of waiting before He releases that "due season" (a season of elevation and favor) talked about in 1 Peter 5:6. God does this for our own good. He is simply developing within us the character that we need in order to operate in the place of influence He is taking us to. And guess what God is using to develop within you such character? Trials and tribulations. It's funny how so many people within the church today equate hard times with divine punishment, believing that if a person is experiencing difficulty in some area of their life (finances, health, etc.) then that is an indication that God is displeased with them. Many people overlook James 1:2-3, which says,

> "Dear brothers and sisters, when troubles come your way, consider it an opportunity for great joy. For you know that when your faith is tested, your endurance has a chance to grow." (NLT)

It may sound strange, but the gift God gives you as a result of your seed is first a problem, something that may look like a setback in life, that which James refers to as a "chance to grow" character. The hardship and difficulty you are experiencing is not a form of punishment; it is really an *opportunity*, a *chance* to be developed by God into a person capable of handling greatness. That's why James said rejoice rather than complain. You have been enrolled into The Academy of Greatness on a full scholarship. Without this opportunity you won't be able to grow, and without growth you won't be able to receive the blessing. Learn what God is trying to teach you in your season of waiting. Learn to rejoice, hold your tongue, employ and speak faith, deal with conflict, and handle the very things God is equiping you to handle. God is by your side. He is not going to let you go under. You are in Greatness School, being prepared for something huge.

LIFE'S INSTRUCTION MANUAL

Another thing God is going to do in you as a result of sowing into His Kingdom is give you the ability to understand His Word when you read it. It is important to mention that this form of understanding is a divine gift. Jesus explained to His disciples in Matthew 13:10-11, "His disciples came and asked him, 'Why do you use parables when you talk to the people?' He replied, 'You are permitted to understand the secrets of the Kingdom of Heaven, but others are not'" (NLT). In 2 Thessalonians 2:11 reveals to us that God will place a veil of spiritual blindness over the eyes of those who refuse to receive the truth. Basically, spiritual sight is given to certain people; the flesh can't interpret the Word of God and glean divine revelation from it. God has to give you this ability. God gives us this ability so that we can understand His Word thoroughly and live by it. Why do you need this particular gift? Because the Bible is filled with instructions for living that guarantee success in every area.

Experts tell us that if we read ten minutes a day, we will increase our self-value significantly; and yet, I've heard many people claim they don't have time to read. Many people say they don't have time to read the Bible, but they have time to read blog posts that cover senseless topics, twitter posts, gossip columns, watch mindless Youtube videos and other useless things. Instead, the God will begin to move on your heart to pick up His Word and study it, which is a sign that God is developing your understanding so that it will be able to match the level of blessing He is about to give you (2 Timothy 2:15).

God gave the Bible an unusual name. He said,

> "Study this Book of Instruction continually. Meditate on it day and night so you will be sure to obey everything written in it. Only then will you prosper and succeed in all you do." (Joshua 1:8, NLT)

God called the Bible a book of instructions that point you in the direction of success in life. God's picture of success is one where you are prospering financially, bodily (in your health), and spiritually according to 3 John 1:2. We're not blessed if we have wealth but not health. You can't enjoy all of your wealth when you're in that position. God's blessing also comes free of mental turmoil and sorrow as revealed in Proverbs 10:22 (and by *blessing*, Solomon means the favor of God). So, with this revelation, we understand this principle: When you invest more time into studying God's Word, learning how to live according to God's precepts and commandments, learning what and what not to do according to God's written instructions, "you will make your own way prosperous." Prosperity won't come from just praying for it (that's the starting point), and it won't come because you began to wish for it; it will come because you invested time into acquiring knowledge of how to live according to God's "Book of Instruction". And it's because of this knowledge that you knew to avoid the pitfalls that lead to poverty and failure and you knew how to create and capitalize on the opportunities that lead to successful living. God did give us an instruction manual for this thing called "life": it's the Bible. It's in your hand...or on your shelf collecting dust. You just need to pick it up, dust it off and then read it. Pursue the wisdom contained therein. The alternative? Well, I will allow Solomon tell you what will happen should you choose not to read the instruction manual (the Bible). This is what God said He will do to those who ignore His instructions:

> "You ignored my advice and rejected the correction I offered. So I will laugh when you are in trouble! I will mock you when disaster overtakes you—when calamity overtakes you like a storm, when disaster engulfs you like a cyclone, and anguish and distress overwhelm you. 'When they cry for help, I will not answer. Though they anxiously search for me, they will not find me. For they hated knowledge and chose not to fear the LORD. They rejected my advice and paid no attention when I corrected them. Therefore, they must eat the bitter fruit of living their own way, choking on their own schemes.'" (Proverbs 1:25-31, NLT).

God will laugh at you. He will sit back and let you fall due to your pride and arrogance in thinking you don't need His instructions because you can figure things out on your own. Ignore God's "Book of Instruction" and not only will God ignore your prayers, but you'll be premeditating your own failure and destruction. Many people are where they are not because they "fell on hard times," but because they decided not to pursue wisdom and understanding from God's Word and have chosen therefore to bring calamity upon their own heads; this pertains to religious people as well; for many in the church ignore the principles of God's Word even while praying earnestly for blessings, and it's the "lack of knowledge" that is causing them to be destroyed, not their lack of prayer. When you *know* differently you will *do* differently.

When you sow into God's Kingdom, He will release wisdom and revelations that attract wealth. Like Peter, Jesus will tell you when and where to cast your net in order to get the fish. God will tell you when and where to invest in order to reap a blessing. God will reveal to you some hidden talent, some gift or hidden treasure buried on the inside of you that can and will release extraordinary wealth into your hands. Imagine God becoming your financial coach. Imagine the Holy Spirit becoming your business partner. What do you think you can accomplish with Him as your advisor? This is how God is repaying you for helping to finance His earthly agenda: He is coaching you directly into wealth strategies and leading you to resources and financial blessings that have been hidden from others; you just have to be willing to follow His every instruction no matter how big or small (1 Corinthians 2:9-16).

THE LAND OF MORE THAN ENOUGH

When the children of Israel were blessed by God to escape from their captivity in Egypt, God instructed them regarding how they were going to receive the land that had been promised to their forefathers. God told the Israelites where to go, what to do, what to touch and what not to touch. God gave them victory over their enemies and spread their name and reputation among the surrounding nations. God's will was for the Israelites to enter into the Promised Land (land of Canaan), which He described as a land flowing with milk and honey. As long as the Israelites remained in the desert, God supernaturally provided for them. God provided water for them from a rock, manna from heaven, and He even placed an anointing on their clothes so that they wouldn't wear out. Everything they received, they had received supernaturally. But the Bible says the day the Israelites crossed over the Jordan River and into the land of Canaan and then ate the produce of the land, that's when the manna stopped falling, that's when the anointing lifted off of their clothes, and that's when the water stopped flowing out of that rock (Joshua 5:12). Why? It's because there was no longer a need to provide food and water and clothing for the Israelites supernaturally being that they were now in a place that was filled with natural springs for water, with fertile land where they could actually grow their own food and feed their livestock, and they had the resources to make their own clothes. You don't need a miracle to pay your bills when you have the money in your bank account to pay them, and you don't need a miracle to provide food on the table when you have the money to purchase food. You don't need a miracle to purchase a house when you have the finances to do so. What God is trying to do is get you into a position where you live in the place of abundance so that you won't be in perpetual need of a miracle.

Miracles are to be a sign to unbelievers, but favor is designed for the Believer. Favor is more than a miracle; it is the supernatural positioning of a person by God into a place of influence, power, wealth and resources. God desires that we be reservoirs of blessings, not spiritual beggars. David, in Psalm 23, spoke of the overflowing cup; this is a reference to favor. This is the final blessing God will bestow upon you when you are a sower into His Kingdom: after undergoing your season of waiting and preparation, He is going to lead you into a place of favor where you will walk in such blessings that people will be attracted to you—and the God that you serve—because of the blessings pouring from your life.

In this season of transitioning, God is causing you to grow and mature spiritually. He's teaching you how to walk in a higher level of awareness and responsibility. He's now transforming you as a person so that you'll be able to handle the full load of the blessing He has for you. This blessing is one where you'll be the lender and not the borrower, above and not beneath, the head and not the tail; this is a wealthy place where you will owe to men only the love that God has given you rather than money; it's a place where you'll have streams of income flowing into your life enabling you to be generous in every occasion. Let God take you there.

If you want to reach your land of destiny, the Promised Land God predestined for you to dwell in, then simply pray this prayer (no, there's no magic involved in this process; but if you declare out loud with me these words, you'll take the most important step on this journey: you'll begin to change your perspective, which will usher you into a new season):

> Dear Heavenly Father, I thank you for your love, your mercy, and your grace. I thank you for sending your Son, Jesus the Christ, to die on the cross for my sins. Through Christ Jesus, I have been redeemed from the hands of Satan and his agents. I thank you that through Christ Jesus I have been made an heir to your precious promises outlined in your Word. All of your promises are *yes* and *amen* in my life. Your Word says in 2 Corinthians 8:9 that Jesus took my poverty upon His back and became poor so that I might be rich. Your Word says in Proverbs 10:22 that your blessing makes us rich and adds no sorrow to it. I confess today that lack is not your will for my life. I confess today that poverty is not your will for my life. I thank you that you desire that I receive your best for my life and for my family. For you stated in Psalms 112 that when a person fears, honor and respects you, that person will have wealth and riches in their household and their righteousness will endure forever; and not only that, but their children and their grandchildren will walk in these blessings as an inheritance. I denounce poverty and lack. I denounce any spiritual authority given to the ene-

my, Satan, over my family bloodline through agreements with demons made by my parents and ancestors. I repent of sin and iniquity, including injustices that may have been committed against others by my loved-ones and passed down iniquity. I denounce witchcraft and any and all occult activity in my life and in my household. I repent if I've withheld your tithe and I commit today to tithing from all increase that you bless me to receive. I repent of sin and command every demon who has been given an assignment to keep me in bondage to release your grip on my life and go back to the pits of hell from whence you came. I am the property of God. Father, give me a clean heart and the right spirit. Let my heart delight in your Word. Give me a desire to live for you and obey you in all things. I repent of the spirit of rebellion and stubbornness and I thank you for a spirit of humility, gratitude, and thankfulness. Today, I thank you for giving me the heart of a servant and for giving me a heart to sow into your Kingdom. Today, I thank you for meeting my needs according to your riches in glory. Today, I thank you for my daily bread and my daily provisions. Today, I declare that my money is your property. I am not under the authority, power, and control of money (of Mammon). Money is my servant and you, Father, are my master. You gave money to me and entrusted me with it. As a sign of my covenant with you, I am a tither. Thank you for blessing me to be able to give. Father, I ask that you place seed into my hands that I might sow more into your Kingdom. Father, I ask that you give me wisdom. Father, I pray that you give me ideas of witty inventions and ideas that will generate wealth in my life and that you will send coaches, mentors, and prophets to guide me even as your Holy Spirit speaks to my heart concerning your will for my life. Speak to me even as I read your Word, and provide me with your revelation and understanding. I thank you that I am blessed, prosperous, wealthy, the lender and not the borrower, the head and not the tail, above and not beneath. I thank you that you are developing my character and maturing me so that I may dwell in the place of abundance that you've predestined for me to dwell in. I was created by you to succeed, to prosper, to be great and do great things in the earth for your glory. I no longer have a poverty mentality, but I accept my divine destiny. I am free from yesterday and ready for your will. I declare and decree that it's already done in Jesus name, amen.

About The Author

Timothy Flemming, Jr. was born on July 12, 1979, in Atlanta, Georgia to Timothy and Virginia Flemming, Sr. Timothy Flemming, Jr. is the youngest of three.

Timothy Flemming, Jr. is an ordained minister. He entered the ministry in 1995.

Timothy is an accomplished writer, having won numerous poetry contests and creative writing contests - the latest being the 2005 Famous Poets Convention held in Reno, Nevada. There, Timothy walked away with the $25,000 grand prize winning, beating poets from all over the world. Timothy is also the author of several books: *Prophetic Patterns in the Bible*, *Exposing the Great Deception*, and *One Giant Away*. In addition to this, Timothy is also a playwright, having written and produced several plays.

Timothy is the founder of T&J Publishers, a Christian-based book publishing company that strives to provide a voice to authors with a positive message.

Timothy Flemming, Jr. is a devoted family man. He married his soul mate, Jackie Flemming, in 2003. He is also a father of three: Timothy Flemming, III; Timera JaNae Flemming, and Jeremiah Flemming.

To contact author, send requests to:
TimFlemm99@gmail.com
www.TimothyFlemmingJr.com